KINGDOM
DRIVEN

The Definitive Guide For How Driven
Christian Men Can Dominate In Life

JOSH KHACHADOURIAN

JOSH KHACHADOURIAN

© 2024 by Josh Khachadourian - www.standard59.com
Printed in the United States of America
Cover design and artwork by Justin Stewart - www.onwrd.io.
Book Formatting and Additional Graphics by Lyss - www.thelovelylyss.com
All rights reserved. No part of this publication may be reproduced, stored in a retrieval system, or transmitted in any form or by any means without the prior written permission of the author/publisher. The exception is brief quotations.

ISBN: 978-1-7345493-3-1

Scripture Quotations Unless otherwise indicated, all Scripture quotations are taken from NEW AMERICAN STANDARD BIBLE®, Copyright © 1960,1962,1963,1968, 1971,1972,1973,1975,1977,1995 by The Lockman Foundation. Used by permission."

Scripture Quotations labeled AMP are from taken from the Amplified® Bible (AMP), Copyright © 2015 by The Lockman Foundation. Used by permission. lockman.org

Scripture Quotations labeled Wuest Translation are from The New Testament, an expanded translation by Kenneth S. Wuest. Copyright Wm. B. Eerdmans Publishing Co. 1961. All rights reserved.

BE THE MAN YOU ARE CREATED TO BE!

Listen to the Raising The Standard Podcast to Get Weekly Motivation for the Kingdom Driven Man

LEADERSHIP, MINDSET AND DEVELOPMENT FOR THE KINGDOM MAN

Listen Today on Your Favorite Podcast Platform

DISCOVER JESUS AS THE STANDARD FOR MASCULINITY

The world is wrestling over the definition of manhood and masculinity. Discover how Jesus sets **The Standard** for you as a man.

GET THE STANDARD

HERE'S WHAT'S INSIDE

PART I

DESTINED FOR DOMINION

- 22 — DESIGNED FOR DOMINION
- 24 — THE DOMINION MANDATE
- 30 — GET A G.D.V.

PART II

KNOW YOUR ENEMIES

- 38 — THE ENEMIES IN YOUR ENVIRONMENT
- 46 — IDENTIFYING THE RESISTANCE
- 54 — GETTING OUT OF THE GAP
- 60 — THE WAY FORWARD

PART III

THE KINGDOM DRIVEN ORDER

68	FROM CHAOS TO ORDER
72	ALIGN: ALIGNING WITH YOUR IDENTITY
80	DESIGN: DESIGNING YOUR LIFE
90	WEAPONIZE: THE WARRIORS MINDSET
96	OPTIMIZE: OPTIMIZING YOUR FAITH, FAMILY, FITNESS AND FINANCES

PART IV

UPGRADE YOUR ENVIRONMENT

114	TRUE TRANSFORMATION
118	THE MISSING INGREDIENT
121	WHAT'S NEXT?

HERE'S HOW TO WORK WITH ME TO IMPLEMENT A SYSTEM AND BECOME POWERFUL IN YOUR FAITH, WIN WITH YOUR FAMILY, ELEVATE YOUR FITNESS, AND MULTIPLY YOUR FINANCES.

Hey Man of God,

Josh K here.

I have one goal with this book: to give you the information you need to be the man God has called you to be so you can:

- ☑ **SMASH UNBELIEF**
- ☑ **DESTROY MEDIOCRITY**
- ☑ **SUCCEED IN YOUR ASSIGNMENTS**
- ☑ **ASCEND IN YOUR SPHERE OF INFLUENCE**
- ☑ **FULFILL YOUR DOMINION MANDATE**

All for the purpose of expanding the Kingdom of God while wreaking havoc on the kingdom of darkness without sacrificing your family, wealth or health.

To accomplish this, you will have to win in the following areas.

FAITH
Get clarity on how to Be the Man God calls you to be so you can reach your full potential

FAMILY
Be the leader in your marriage and family

FITNESS
Optimize your fitness, steward your temple, and manage your energy

FINANCE

Build your kingdom wealth war map to accomplish your vision and leave a legacy

As Christian men living in the business world, we have unique challenges, whether you are an entrepreneur building a business, a corporate executive navigating your career, punching a clock in a 9 to 5 or you're immersed in a competitive sales environment working to maximize your income. I have walked in your shoes and have experienced the challenges of managing competing priorities with life and work. Balancing being a husband, showing up as a father, and crushing it at work is easier said than done. Most men do well in one or maybe two of these areas, but it's rare to see men who dominate across all these areas of life.

In this book, I am giving away the strategies and tactics I have used in my own life and the lives of the men I work with so you can avoid the most common pitfalls, obtain the breakthrough, and sustain the victory.
The origin of the information you are about to access is based on Kingdom principles. God establishes order with eternal principles and laws that can not be violated. It is mission-critical to order your life, guide your family, build your business, and steward your temple in alignment with this blueprint found in Scripture.

I often hear from men asking me how they can get more help to achieve personal breakthrough, and fully implement and optimize what you're about to learn from this book in their lives.

So, if you want me to help you 1:1,

All you have to do is shoot me an email to Josh@standard59.com and message me the word 'KINGDOM' and I'll get you all of the details.

LEAD. FIGHT. WIN.

Josh K

INTRODUCTION

It's a normal day. I am starting my day at sunrise in the Lord's presence. I am full of peace, inner contentment, and revelation of what the Lord is showing me today. I have energy, I am focused, full of faith and operating at full intention.

Later today, my wife and I will sit down for coffee, share each other's dreams, pray for each other, and ask how we can serve and support each other.

Our kids are serving the Lord. I am winning at work and building a legacy for my family. I am in shape and have the energy to meet the challenges of the day. I have built lifelong friendships and have a support network of brothers inside Standard 59 who I would take a bullet for, and they would do the same for me. All men need a circle of friends they can count on for support, counsel, brotherhood, and fun.

It's not that I don't face challenges, fire drills, or tests. It's that I am equipped to operate from peace with wisdom, walking in partnership with God despite the challenges I face in life.

If I rewind the clock 15 years…

I was a Christian, but my days were very different. I was running and gunning, wired and tired, and the stress of work was overwhelming some days. Honestly, I was not in the best place in my marriage. Somewhere along the way, we shifted from newlyweds to roommates.

So, I hyper-focused on work or found my escape in the gym. I would bury the pain, the disappointment, and the hurt through my medication of choice. For me, it was working hard building my career and spending hours in the gym building my body. It was easy to hide behind 'being busy' just enough to get by and not face the reality of how I felt like a failure even though my bank account was growing.

On the outside, things have never been better if status and money are your standards. Working in New York City was influencing me. I was surrounded by wealth, outward appearance, the lust of the eyes, the flesh, and the pride of life. When you are living in what feels like a pressure cooker, it can feel like there's no way out.

Where I am operating from today in my relationship with the Lord has revolutionized my life. My marriage is thriving, I have strong relationships with my children, and I am fueled by purpose in my work, expanding the Kingdom and building a legacy for my family.

What changed? How did I go from experiencing chaos, feeling overwhelmed and like there was never enough time in the day to pivoting to peace and prosperity in every area of my life?

All men have a conflict they must conquer in their leadership journey. There are barriers to overcome, obstacles to avoid, and giants to kill. This war must be won, and territory must be taken on the journey to being the man God created us to be.

Our greatest fear is that we will not fulfill our potential and live out the unique call of God on our lives. But, despite this fear, most men have leveled off and are suffering from MEDIOCRITY.

- ☑ **DISCONNECTED FROM THEIR PURPOSE**
- ☑ **DISTRACTED, LACKING FOCUS, AND MISSING A MISSION**
- ☑ **DEFLECTING RESPONSIBILITY IN AREAS THEY ARE CALLED TO BE THE LEADER**
- ☑ **DEFENDING WHERE THEY ARE IN LIFE BY MINIMIZING, MAKING EXCUSES AND BLAME-SHIFTING INSTEAD OF TAKING RESPONSIBILITY**

The core conflict in your life needs to be identified, and you must be equipped to conquer it. My story is a journey of self-study, the wisdom of mentors, the counsel of coaches, and more trial and error than I care to admit. Along the way, I discovered Kingdom principles derived from ancient wisdom and proven by modern science that turned into deliberate practices and formed a framework I call the Kingdom Driven Order.

I have made it my mission to share this with other men. I have been teaching the Kingdom Driven Order within a coaching group I run called The Standard 59 Mastermind. Throughout this book, I will reference the mastermind and some of the practices we use.

The men in our brotherhood are shedding the shame of past events and experiences that kept them trapped in a false identity and living in the chains of mediocrity. One of the first things we do inside our brotherhood is ALIGN you with your real identity. When this happens, we see men take the first step into the freedom of knowing who they are created to be and operating from a new identity with a new perspective.

Next, we DESIGN our lives to take dominion in the areas we are called to occupy and advance. This starts with taking dominion over our day and exercising responsibility for deliberately designing our lives. We understand that we are in a battle and are not fighting flesh and blood. To take dominion and advance the Kingdom of God in life, we put on the mindset of a warrior, armor up, and WEAPONIZE for the fight. On our leadership journey, we are committed to training and deliberate practice to OPTIMIZE our entire being, spirit, soul, and body.

We don't use guess work or hard work, we follow a framework that orders our lives.

THE
KINGDOM DRIVEN
ORDER

ALIGN

DESIGN

DOMINION

OPTIMIZE

WEAPONIZE

There is power in implementing order in your life with a well-designed strategy. As men, we build business plans, create strategies and systems, and then execute. Investing time, energy, and focus into building your business and developing your plans for life is common practice.

But when it comes to investing our energy into building a plan to ensure we grow spiritually strong, lead our families, and do the things that carry eternal value, most men just 'wing it.' If you want to take dominion in life, it starts with being intentional.

In this book, you will identify God's will for your life and become aware of the enemies opposing you from moving into the highest call God has for you. Discover the most common pitfalls that trap and trip men up before you get equipped with the tools to implement the Kingdom-Driven Order into your life.

Congratulations on taking action to discover how to get clarity and be the man God created you to be so you can embrace your dominion mandate and dominate every area of your life. Let's get started!

To learn more about the Standard 59 Mastermind visit
https://www.standard59.com/mastermind

ARE YOU KINGDOM DRIVEN?

Jesus preached the message of the Kingdom of God. The Kingdom is not one-dimensional and is too expansive to attempt to exhaust here. To get us on the same page, I will borrow a simple definition of the Kingdom of God from my friend and best-selling author, Frank Viola.

"The Kingdom Of God is the manifestation of God's ruling presence. Jesus Christ is the rule of God. Jesus Christ is the presence of God. He is the manifestation of the Kingdom. Wherever he is, there the kingdom is."

As a son of God and disciple of Jesus Christ, you carry the Kingdom. You are designed to display God's image to a broken and fallen world. The message of the Kingdom is good news. It carries solutions to problems we face, solutions for relationships, business, and life. My friend Richard Furlow states that:

"The Kingdom of God is the rule and reign of Jesus Christ through His people on earth and in heaven."

This means you have a specific and unique role to play in the expression of the Kingdom of God in and through you.

Being Kingdom-Driven is about being relentless in your pursuit of God's highest calling for man. It's not about settling or being content with a 'ticket to heaven.' It's all about reaching your full potential and developing into your full stature so you can receive and give God His full inheritance.

DOES THIS SOUND LIKE YOU?

- ☑ You're ready to step into and live out your purpose with power and wisdom.

- ☑ You want to make an impact within your sphere of influence.

- ☑ You are ready to understand your gifts and calling to add value to those around you.

- ☑ You want to solve problems and serve people in the marketplace by partnering with God.

- ☑ You want to fulfill the call and potential that God has given you and stand before Him at the end of your life, knowing you played full out so you can hear the Lord say: "Well done my good and faithful servant."

To be faithful means to be "full of faith." As you are reading this book right now, you may be in a place where you have lost your vision and your way and cannot confidently say that you are full of faith. Or you may be in a place right now where you are full of strength, have a vision for the future, and are ready to run. Regardless of which man you most identify with right now, the purpose of this book is to light the fuse that will cause you to walk into your purpose with explosive power, take your territory, and be the man God created you to be. But no man can walk in his purpose with power if he does not understand what was in the heart of God when He created man.

Many men have bought into the lie that they must check their ambition at the door. They have a distorted view of humility and wrestle over what they really want, how they think they are supposed to be, and what they're allowed to do.

Let's liberate you from the chains of false humility, the lies about your ambition, and the scarcity thinking that keeps you playing small!

> *"Engage in business until I come."*
> - Jesus, Luke 19:13

PART I:
DESTINED FOR DOMINION

DESIGNED FOR DOMINION

You want more because you are created in the image and likeness of the CREATOR. In Genesis 1:28, God handed dominion over the earth to the first man. Even though Adam messed up and forfeited his authority to the enemy in Genesis chapter 3, it doesn't change God's original intent for you.

This desire for dominion is in your DNA. This inner fire is imparted at the cellular level. The drive to expand, create, build, produce, and prosper in everything you put your hand to is God-given.

If you want:
- ☑ **MORE POWER**
- ☑ **MORE PURPOSE**
- ☑ **MORE PASSION**
- ☑ **MORE PEACE**
- ☑ **MORE PROSPERITY**

It's because God encoded this desire into your DNA.

If you want to walk in unbroken fellowship with your creator, hear Him with clarity, demonstrate power, multiply everything you touch, impart your strength, and bring solutions in partnership with God… vs. feeling disconnected and cloudy, missing direction in life.
It's because of the **DOMINION MANDATE**.

If you want a thriving marriage that's on fire, built with love and respect, where you serve, support, and minister to each other…vs. endless arguments, conflict, and feeling trapped in a sexless marriage with no connection.

It's because of the **DOMINION MANDATE**.

If you want to be the leader of your home, guiding your children to grow in life, serve the Lord, and see them go farther than you… vs. being checked out, embarrassed, or ashamed of how your children behave.
It's because of the **DOMINION MANDATE**.

If you want to expand in business, provide solutions, serve others, make money, save money, spend money, and give money… vs. living paycheck to paycheck, in debt with seemingly no way out.
It's because of the **DOMINION MANDATE**.

If you want to operate at full energy, be physically strong, capable of protecting yourself, your family, and defending the weak… vs. feeling exhausted and being overweight, with limited mobility.
It's because of the **DOMINION MANDATE**.

"I alone came in order that they might be possessing life, and that they might be possessing it in superabundance."
- Jesus

John 10:10
Wuest Translation

THE DOMINION MANDATE
THE 5-FOLD CALLING OF MAN

God created man in His own image, in the image of God He created him; male and female He created them. God blessed them; and God said to them, "Be fruitful and multiply, and fill the earth, and subdue it; and rule over the fish of the sea and over the birds of the sky and over every living thing that moves on the earth."

Genesis 1:27-28

You are made in God's image and His likeness, you are commissioned to be an 'imager' of God. His intention was that you would operate like Him and be His representative on the earth in every sphere of life. What follows next is a mandate to man. The commands that Adam received from the Lord reveal our destiny, our design, and the way God created us to function as men in the earth.

When God creates man, He blesses him and gives him five distinct commands. This is the Dominion Mandate.

#1 BE FRUITFUL
#2 MULTIPLY
#3 REPLENISH THE EARTH
#4 CONQUER AND SUBDUE
#5 TAKE DOMINION OVER THE EARTH

Traditional teaching has looked at these commands as only pertaining to natural and physical realities. But God always starts in the spiritual realm first when demonstrating a natural reality. When you see this, these mandates will go far beyond just starting a family and repopulating the earth. Let's break these down and see how they apply to our lives right here and right now.

ORIGIN DICTATES DESTINY

When God places Adam and Eve in the Garden of Eden and charges them with the Dominion Mandate, the first thing He does is bless them. The blessing God pronounces over them fills them with the strength, power, and favor to succeed in life. Immediately following this blessing, God issues a fivefold mandate.

DOMINION MANDATE #1 BE FRUITFUL

Bearing fruit can also be translated as growing and increasing. God intends for you to grow and mature. This pattern would have also been observed in the garden's plant life. Everything God creates is meant to grow. The concept of potential is hidden within the garden and encoded in your spiritual DNA. The command to grow, increase, expand, and bear fruit is the result of the release of the potential God placed within you as a man.

You are a new creation as a follower of Jesus and you carry latent power translated as potential within your spirit. As a man who is created as an image bearer and representative of God on the earth, you are given a unique assignment and individual calling. In order to fulfill the call and fully express the potential you carry, you must develop and grow so you can bear fruit in your life.

Bearing fruit can also be considered as having results in life. When Jesus is hungry and stops by a fig tree to find fruit but finds none, He curses the tree, see Mark 11 for the whole story. The Lord expects a return on His investment and desires that you will produce fruit. Bearing fruit represents personal growth in our lives as men in pursuing and fulfilling our Kingdom assignments.

DOMINION MANDATE #2 MULTIPLY

You have been given a mandate to multiply. This call to duplicate and reproduce goes beyond physical reproduction. Growth is accelerated through multiplication, and for multiplication to align with God's design, there must first be maturity. All fruit must grow and produce the seeds inwardly before reproducing outwardly. This mirrors your leadership journey: inward development precedes outward impact.

It is important for you to understand that what you carry and have to offer is not just for you. You have the ability and are commanded to multiply. Multiplication is part of your design as a man. You are to multiply the things that you touch. The Kingdom principle of stewardship is a charge to manage and multiply. A man who exhibits stewardship over his life will always multiply his resources and have demonstrated results. The purpose of the fruit is to multiply into more fruit. The Lord commands increase through multiplication. Your gifts and talents are not for you alone. Your mandate is to multiply.

DOMINION MANDATE #3: REPLENISH

The command to replenish is also translated as to fill or be full, 'to fulfill.' The Hebrew word carries the meaning of ordaining or consecrating for service to God. There is something holy about replenishing. It is connected to a larger purpose and service. Within the garden, there was an abundant supply of every resource needed. In the Kingdom of God, there is an abundant supply of all things available to us. This requires you to take on the mind of Christ and see through an abundance mindset.

In the first Dominion Mandate, we see fruitfulness as growing within yourself. It's a journey of growth in all areas of your life. In Dominion Mandate Two, we see the next stage is to multiply and duplicate what you're carrying, so you have for yourself, but you also have enough to give away. This is followed by a mandate to replenish.

It is a continual cycle of filling. It's a continual abundance of resources and supplies that never runs out. I have enough for myself, and enough to give away in the sphere of influence I'm called to. I also have the ability to replenish.

In Ephesians 5:18, the apostle Paul instructs us to be filled with the Holy Spirit. It is a verb that implies a continuous infilling. It's not a one-time filling; it is something that we are to do continually. It's a replenishment, an abundance, and an overflow that is available to us.

DOMINION MANDATE #4 SUBDUE

The fourth mandate is to subdue or conquer the earth. The word subdue can be translated as conquer and subjugate using force. Adam was appointed to this physical and spiritual sphere called the Garden of Eden. He was to subdue the land. He was given the authority to rule over it as king of the earth under the headship of God.

We can connect subduing to the command God gives Adam to 'keep' the garden, which means to guard it. You are to guard the territory you occupy from all enemy intrusion. God empowered Adam with the strategy and strength to watch over the garden. God has empowered you with the strength to protect and watch over what He has entrusted to you from all enemy attacks.

DOMINION MANDATE #5 TAKE DOMINION

The Lord commanded Adam to take dominion over the earth. Dominion means to rule, dominate, and exercise authority over. This mandate charges man as a caretaker of his territory. Adam was entrusted to care for the garden and everything within it. Even the animals would be under his jurisdiction. God's mandate to take dominion in your life is connected with the assignment in the sphere of influence He has placed you in. Taking dominion in life means ruling over your circumstances and not being ruled by things that have no God-given authority in your life.

Taking dominion over territory and learning to dominate what you are called to do is not to be confused with dominating people. The leadership model Jesus provides us with is servant leadership, which is diametrically opposed to domination over others. Adam is given a mandate to dominate systems and spheres.

Man's first vocation was as a gardener. The sphere and means of man's full development are to take place within a garden—a place where life grows. Man will be charged with unleashing the garden's full potential as he learns to work in this field. Adam was charged with exercising dominion over the garden. But because he sins within the garden, he is driven out.

The New Testament reality is that you are the garden. Just as Adam was charged to exercise dominion within the garden, you must exercise dominion over yourself. Self leadership is the qualifier before you are given leadership over others. Every man must learn to lead himself before he is qualified to lead his world.

The DOMINION MANDATE is your calling and destiny. God's intention for you to represent Him in the earth has never changed.

THE DOMINION MANDATE SUMMARY

The first step to taking dominion in your life is understanding God's Goal for you is GROWTH. Pursue personal growth in every area of your life and be intentional about your spiritual development. These are not just commands, these mandates are mindsets.

BEAR FRUIT
You are designed to make an impact and deliver results

MULTIPLY
You were created to multiply what you put your hand to

REPLENISH
You possess the power to create and reproduce

SUBDUE
You overcome resistance by exercising your God-ordained strength

TAKE DOMINION
You were created to rule and dominate in life

Taking dominion is LEADERSHIP. As a man, you were created to be a leader. You lead in life by first leading yourself and courageously translating your convictions into bold actions.

Taking dominion is dominating in the sphere of influence God called you to. When God places you in an assignment, all the resources needed to succeed are provided. Your responsibility is to develop the potential within you through partnership with God.

Taking dominion is not dominating people; it's dominating ourselves and demonstrating self-mastery in every area. In the Kingdom, we lead people with the heart of a servant.

GET A G.D.V.
GOD'S WILL IS SYNONYMOUS WITH SUCCESS

God had a clear vision when He created man and placed him in the earth to dominate it. You must have a God Driven Vision or what I refer to as a GDV for your life as you journey with God as a co-creator. This starts with understanding and accepting that God's will for your life is synonymous with success.

When The Lord commissions Joshua, He gives the following instructions:

"This book of the law shall not depart from your mouth, but you shall meditate on it day and night, so that you may be careful to do according to all that is written in it; for then you will make your way prosperous, and then you will have success.

Joshua 1:8

Joshua will make his way prosperous, and he will have success when he does all the Lord commanded him to do. You cannot be successful if you do not define success. Success is not measured by your bank account, the square footage of your house, or the number of cars in your driveway. For all men, God's goal is growth, and the manifestation of that growth is to be in alignment with God's specific will for your life. For Joshua, his success and prosperity were linked to leading the nation of Israel into the Promised Land, also known as their inheritance.

Your Promised Land is the place in life that you are called to occupy; this is God's will for you. Success for Kingdom Driven Men is executing the Lord's plan in partnership with Him for your life. Success is being in and doing God's will for your life.

EVERY MAN IS CREATED TO SOLVE A PROBLEM.

Whenever God wants to solve a problem, He uses a man. Every man of God we read about in scripture who fulfills God's will carries a solution to a problem. When God wants to promote you, He raises you up with a solution. He will even create a problem that only you have the solution for.

Without a famine, Joseph would not have been chosen to offer his consulting and wisdom to Pharaoh and preserve the nation of Israel. Joseph was promoted from the pit to the prison to the palace because he carried the solution to a problem.

Moses received training in Egypt's systems and schools, and then he was extracted and taken to the wilderness to be prepared to deliver his nation. He would not only lead the nation to liberation from slavery but also use his business training from his time in Egypt to govern, construct the Tabernacle, and build the economy.

Daniel's gift of dream interpretation brought him before kings to solve problems that only he had the solution for. Developing his gifting and walking in integrity and obedience opened doors to promotion and leadership within Babylon.

Whether it's a priest, a prophet, a king, a teacher, or a businessman God uses men to bring solutions to their world in their season. The enemy launches a targeted attack on men around their inner ambition and drive to keep you playing small so you don't fully step into being the leader in your life. If you believe you are not allowed to have ambition in life and pursue the dream within your heart, you will experience an inner struggle. You will want to run to hit your targets and crush your goals, and then you will hit the brakes, wondering if you're too driven. Religion messes men up with a distorted message of humility and ambition. If you overestimate your skills and abilities, you get into pride. If you underestimate yourself and deliberately attempt to minimize your value, you get into false humility. True humility results in an accurate assessment of yourself.

Humility is Stability. When you walk in true humility that honors God, it doesn't matter what others think or say about you. You are secure in your identity and can operate from a solid foundation. Pride always comes before a fall.

Ambition is God-given. It's not that you can't have ambition, but it needs to be aligned with God's will for your life. While the Bible warns us about 'selfish ambition,' there is no blanket warning on being driven. Every man of God pursuing God's will is driven by the vision God placed within them.

A God Driven Vision is not the world's version of staring at your dream sports car on your vision board every morning or using the law of attraction to try and manifest your personal desires into your life. Having a GDV gives you clarity and course direction.

God put a desire within you that you would want to take dominion over circumstances and live a life that reflects His glory and honors Him. When Jesus encounters the man at the pool of Bethsaida He looks him directly in the eyes and asks,

WHAT DO YOU WANT?

As you receive and develop your GDV, you must be honest with yourself and God about what you want. God imparts desires within your spirit that fit your design, disposition, and gift mix. Psalm 37:4 promises that when you "delight yourself in the LORD, He will give you the desires of your heart." Developing your GDV will require your commitment and trust, which result from walking with God. He is the one who shapes the vision, aligning your desires with His purpose and provision

GOD LOVES GOALS

God loves it when YOU have goals in life. When the disciples run up to Jesus and start arguing over who will be the greatest in the Kingdom, notice what Jesus DOES NOT do.

- ☑ HE NEVER REBUKES THEM FOR ASKING THE QUESTION OF WHO THE GREATEST WILL BE.
- ☑ HE NEVER SAYS THAT'S THE WRONG QUESTION.
- ☑ HE NEVER CORRECTS THE FRAME OF MIND THEY APPROACHED WITH.

I believe Jesus liked the fact that they were thinking this way. It pleases God when we desire the best. When Jesus teaches His disciples servant leadership and states, "Whoever wants to be great…" He is validating their desire for greatness.

God wants you to desire the best, the highest, and the biggest dreams you can dream with Him. He put this drive within you for more. If you're dreaming big - DON'T STOP.

GET A G.D.V. SUMMARY

God's will for your life is synonymous with success. Success for you is being who God called you to be and doing what God called you to do.

Developing a God Driven Vision empowers you to operate with clarity, certainty, and confidence, knowing you are traveling in the right direction to fulfill God's will for your life.

Your God Driven Vision will align with solving problems in your sphere of influence through utilizing your unique skills, talents and spiritual gifts.

Your ambition needs to be aligned with God's desires and a drive to expand the Kingdom of God, not selfish ambitions.

Having goals honors God, who wants the best for you - so dream big dreams with Him and don't settle for less than His perfect will in your life.

Inside the Standard 59 Mastermind, we equip men with the knowledge and training to dream, discover, develop, and deploy a God Driven Vision in their lives. You can learn more at

https://www.standard59.com/mastermind

PART II:
KNOW YOUR ENEMIES

THE ENEMIES IN YOUR ENVIRONMENT
THE ATTACK ON MASCULINITY

You have now been equipped with the knowledge that your masculine inner drive to take dominion in your life, exhibit leadership, and experience growth is downloaded in your DNA. God designed you for leadership. It's at the heart of your dominion mandate. There is a fight raging over your calling to lead in life, and right now, you need to be aware that enemies are working overtime to sabotage God's plan for the world and the role you play. You are under attack, and you must know your enemies.

On your leadership journey, you will face three enemies:

- ☑ SATAN
- ☑ THE WORLD AND ITS SYSTEMS
- ☑ YOURSELF

Just wanting to step into leadership or feeling the call to exhibit dominion over life's challenges doesn't mean you have it. In fact, taking dominion in your faith, family, fitness, and finances is rarely seen in the lives of modern Christian men. Let's identify the enemies that are secretly sabotaging our power and actively working against us from taking dominion in all of the areas we are called to lead.

THE INSTITUTIONAL RELIGIOUS MACHINE

THE ATTACK ON OUR RELATIONSHIP WITH GOD

Many of us are walking around with passed-down views of an angry God who is a demanding judge in the sky, watching down and waiting for us to mess up. We have been programmed by institutional religion that we should view ourselves as 'sinners' and not sons. For many of us, this results in a works-based mindset that keeps us constantly performing, trying hard to modify our behaviors, and leaving us feeling like failures. Incorrect doctrine and teaching, plus our internal wiring to 'work for it,' have us constantly running on a hamster wheel of 'doing' and never arriving. This makes your connection with God cloudy and leaves you in a cycle of shame and never feeling good enough.

In addition, the church doesn't have the greatest track record with issues relating to masculinity. During the Industrial Revolution, men left their homes to go to work and also left the church. This led to a church that catered to women and presented a feminized version of Christianity with an effeminate Jesus. In my book, THE STANDARD: Discovering Jesus as The Standard For Masculinity, I break down how Jesus is man as God intended man to be.

So whether your religious beliefs handed you a God you would never want as a "Father," or your experience presented you with a distant savior that you could never connect with. The religious mindset has proven to be a barrier that keeps men from walking in relationship with God and functioning in their true God-given identity.

THE TOXIC MASCULINITY CULTURE

THE ATTACK ON OUR IDENTITY AND MINDSET

We have been immersed in a culture that hates men. Right now, there is a deliberate attempt to dismantle the nuclear family. The programming through entertainment has presented the 'dopey dad' sitting on the couch with his hand shoved in his pants, 'numb and dumb' while his wife disrespects him and his kids disdain him. He's presented as soft, out of touch, overweight, and he's the butt of every joke.

This sad portrayal of men has morphed into a full frontal assault on what the world has labeled 'toxic masculinity.' The mainstream media machine is working overtime to create a narrative that traditional masculinity is 'toxic.' We have observed a concerted effort to sideline traditional masculine characteristics like leadership, discipline, delayed gratification, work ethic, being physically strong, and using that strength to provide and protect the weak and vulnerable in society. This battle is now raging against children as we are directed to raise our kids like indoor cats, helping them avoid hard work and replace challenges in life with plastic participation trophies.

THE POWERS THAT SHAPE THE NARRATIVE HATE TRADITIONAL MARRIAGE

THE ATTACK ON OUR MARRIAGE AND THE NUCLEAR FAMILY

Family is God's idea, and when done correctly, it serves as a model of how we relate to God and each other. This is why there is a relentless attack on the God-given institution of the nuclear family. The culture has sold men a lie, presenting marriage as a prison and building an industry that makes breaking your vows quick and convenient. Easy access to porn and mainstream soft porn ads of naked women are furiously bombarding you to rewire your desires. This sets you up for a slippery slope of straying from God and your family.

As followers of Jesus, we are called to exemplify holiness and purity in our character and conduct. For every man, this journey begins in the heart. The assault on purity and faithfulness is sown as seeds that present an opportunity for compromise. When the seeds of compromise take root, they yield the fruit of separation and divorce, permanently reshaping family structures and disrupting God's design for the nuclear family. We have been sold the lie that 'the grass is greener on the other side of the fence,' which has created broken families and assaulted God's plan for the image of fathers in the home.

MULTINATIONAL MARKETING MACHINES THAT DRIVE CONSUMERISM CULTURE

THE ATTACK ON OUR ATTENTION

We are facing unprecedented distraction from systems engineered by behavior psychologists to capture our attention and steal our focus. Social Media platforms, marketing agencies, and multinational companies employ the world's smartest people to create platforms and campaigns with the mission of getting you addicted to them. This leads to consumption and comparison, which causes distraction and depression, separating us from our Dominion Mandate.

Sophisticated marketing campaigns appeal to base-level desires of comfort and status that drive you to spend money you don't have to buy things you don't need to impress people you don't know. Like a mouse chasing cheese, the behaviors of the masses have been conditioned to take the bait on cue.

The strategy is to keep you in constant comfort so you sit passively on the sidelines and offer no resistance. During 2020 there were virtually no barriers to getting weed, liquor, or toilet paper from mass-market chain stores while Porn Hub gave out free trials. Meanwhile, attending a gathering with other believers was banned. It's time we take the blindfold off. There are powerful people influenced by dark forces engineering our environment, marketing messages, and offering an unprecedented level of comfort to keep men 'checked out.'

THE ATTACK ON YOUR MASCULINITY

THE ATTACK ON OUR BODIES AND HEALTH

The demasculinization of men is not only being portrayed in the media;

it's showing up in the foods and products we consume. Today's modern man has only a fraction of the testosterone of his grandfather. This is a direct result of our toxic environment. Processed foods are engineered to be addictive and stuffed with more chemicals than a 7th-grade science experiment. If you don't believe me, try reading a food label of the toxic sludge they market to our kids with colorful cartoon characters.

The food supply is literally blowing up, and what's left is processed garbage leaving you looking and feeling like a dumpster fire instead of performing like a king in the earth, made in the image of the creator of the universe.

In addition to dealing with genetically modified food, we now have to navigate the effects of EMF (electromagnetic frequencies) and 5G radiation, which hijack our focus and sap our energy levels.

WE NEED STRONG MEN TO ARISE

We just identified five enemies that are withstanding you at the gates from walking out Biblical manhood and modeling true masculinity. This assault on men is tied to a much deeper and nefarious purpose. As we stated, God operates by principles that, when honored, yield fruit, and when dishonored, come with consequences.

> *"Righteousness exalts a nation,*
> *But sin is a disgrace to any people."*
>
> Proverbs 14:34

'Disgrace' in this verse can also be translated as 'condemnation.' When sin goes unaddressed with no repentance, it brings condemnation, and the consequences will be seen and felt within our culture. When society rejects God, moral absolutes, and natural law it accelerates its path toward judgment and destruction. The rejection of God always leads to the judgment of God.

One of the signs of judgment on a nation is the removal of strong men. When God judges a culture, He removes the leaders. We see this play out repeatedly and explicitly in scripture. When the prophet Isaiah starts his mission, he is commissioned to demonstrate God's mercy by calling the nation of Israel to repent for their rebellion and return to God. If they repent and return they will be established and encounter God's blessing and protection. Because they do not repent, Isaiah prophesies a day of reckoning is coming. In Isaiah chapter 3, we see the consequences that come with this judgment, where God promises to remove the leaders.

"The brave man and the warrior [He is also removing],
The judge and the prophet,
The diviner and the elder,
The captain of fifty and the man of honor,
The counselor and the expert artisan,
And the skillful enchanter.
And I will make mere boys their princes,
And capricious (impulsive, unpredictable) children will rule over them.
And the people will be oppressed,
Each one by another, and each one by his neighbor;
The boy will be arrogant and insolent toward the elder
And the vulgar (common) toward the honorable [person of rank]."

Isaiah 3:2-5 AMP

When the prophet Jeremiah declares judgment against the nations that are oppressing Israel, he states that their mighty men "will become like women" (Jeremiah 50:37). The removal of strong men is directly connected with God's judgment of a nation.

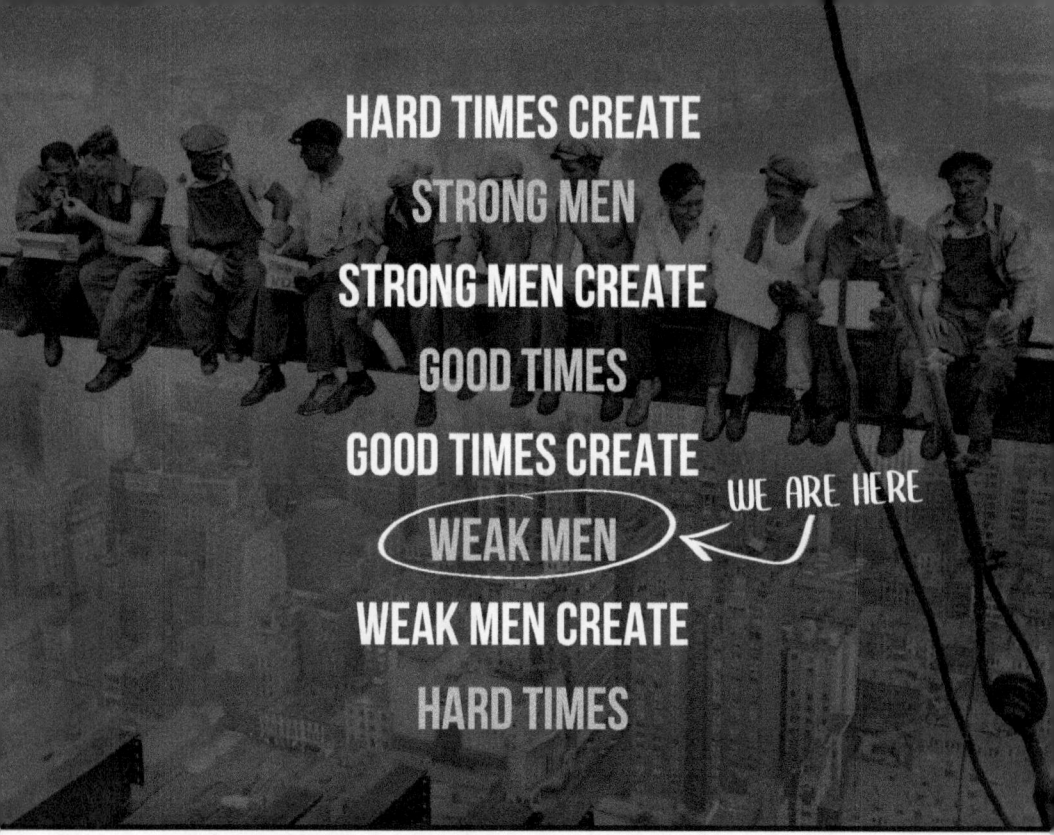

THIS COULDN'T BE MORE TRUE THAN RIGHT NOW.

A look at the current landscape confirms that your masculine identity and leadership face strategic attacks on many cultural fronts today. Dark forces are working to oppose our God-given strengths and ambitions. External systems have been engineered to monopolize your focus and manage your mind. Recognizing these enemies helps clarify the need to safeguard your attention and guard yourself and your family against the enemies seeking to shape your thinking.

You must stand firm in the truth of who you are created to be as a son of the Most High. While the media and even religious doctrines spread misconceptions, our identity remains rooted in the unchanging source of Jesus as our model for true manhood.

Going forward, you will learn to align, design, weaponize, and optimize effectively through the Kingdom Driven Order.

THE ENEMIES IN YOUR ENVIRONMENT SUMMARY

You are facing strategic attacks against your masculine identity, leadership ability, and God-given strengths. These attacks are directly related to the vision God has for men to operate in His image.

Due to religious programming, many men view God as a judge who is hard to please. This leads to a performance mentality that programs you to 'work for it.'

Traditional masculinity has been labeled toxic masculinity. Our culture celebrates instant reward and comfort over leadership, discipline, and delayed gratification.

There is a relentless attack on the God-given institution of the nuclear family. The culture has sold men a lie, presenting marriage as a prison and building an industry that makes breaking your vows quick and convenient.

You are facing unprecedented distraction from systems engineered by behavior psychologists to capture your attention and steal your focus.

Recognizing these enemies is the first step in building self-awareness to overcome the strategies preventing you from stepping into your LEADERSHIP position and operating with PURPOSE and POWER.

IDENTIFYING THE RESISTANCE
WINNING THE WAR WITHIN

Every man "wants" more faith to experience the purpose and power of God in His life, knowing he is maximizing his potential and has the resources to fulfill his calling. And this is where most guys get stuck. Being aware that you are hungry gets you nothing, and having the desire for 'more' is not enough. Due to the religious programming, weak role models, and mixed messages you have likely picked up from other "nice Christian guys," you end up with an internal struggle.

You are hungry for more than you are experiencing right now, but you have to deal with conflicting messages and thoughts about who you're supposed to be and what you should do. The enemy launches a targeted attack on men around their inner ambition and drive. He has carefully constructed false belief systems to indoctrinate Christians that money is the root of all evil, poverty is a virtue, and we should not have a drive to want more. All of these false beliefs keep you from stepping into leadership in your life.

God's goal for you is growth, and it must be your goal as well. But there's a catch: the growth that God wants in your life doesn't happen automatically. There is a CHOICE to be made.

- You never accidentally learned a foreign language
- You never accidentally got shredded
- And you won't accidentally encounter radical spiritual growth and the favor that comes with the abundant life Jesus spoke of

You are created to BE THE MAN who operates in his purpose with power, certainty, and unbreakable confidence. But you must DECIDE and PURSUE.

The question before you right now is, what will you choose?

It's in every great story;

1. Will you take the red pill and unlock life-changing truth, or take the blue pill and stay in the Matrix?

2. Train with a Jedi or sit back as the dark side takes over?

3. Fight Drago on his home turf or take the easy way out? (btw, there is no easy way out....and no shortcut home. If you don't get this reference, it's from Rocky IV - the best one.)

You always have a choice.

Will you embrace the transformation process of conformity to Christ or choose comfort? But what happens every time you decide to step forward and pursue more in life? You hit a wall.

This wall is called RESISTANCE, and you must be equipped with the tools to overcome all resistance in life. In the last chapter, we identified our external enemies, but;

> **THE GREATEST RESISTANCE TO BE OVERCOME IS THE WAR WITHIN.**

IT'S ALL YOUR B.S.

Your belief system (B.S.) shapes the way you see and experience the world. From birth to age 7, you are programmed with life experiences that become hardwired and form your beliefs and internal operating system. Your family's beliefs, attitudes, and traumas were passed down to you and shaped what you see, believe, and how you experience your life. Your internal belief system is the foundation for all of your life's decisions, actions, and reactions.

SALVATION IS THE DOOR

When you commit your life to Jesus and receive salvation, God forgives your sins and brings you back into right standing with Him. The redemptive act of the cross by God on your behalf restores you back to His original intent for man. Receiving your salvation by grace is not the ultimate intention for man, and salvation alone is not God's eternal purpose. Salvation is the door, not the destination.

If you don't understand why and how you get STUCK in the GAP between where God has destined you and where you are today, it's because you were not told what happened when you received your salvation. When you get saved, all of your sins are wiped away, but your old belief system, selfish desires, wounds, patterns, and reactions do not automatically disappear. Your human spirit receives new life in seed form, and this seed contains the blueprint of who you are to be in Christ.

If you are only told Jesus died for your sins, you are missing the tools to align and walk out the Christian life. Without the proper instruction, you may never experience the growth that God intends for you so you can reach your full potential.

Your soul is comprised of your mind, will, and emotions. Your soul still carries your old patterns, reactions, and beliefs. The New Testament instructs us to constantly renew our minds and thinking to transform our soul into the image of God. By rewiring your thoughts and ordering your behavior, you install new habits that align with your new identity. This is how spiritual growth occurs, and you reach full stature, becoming a mature man.

This growth is not guaranteed. This is why the New Testament is full of warnings to Christians to walk worthy of their calling. This means it's possible to be SAVED and STUCK and be FORGIVEN, but FAILING in life. The most frustrating place a man can be is knowing he's meant for more but living with unmet potential.

In the last chapter you became aware of your external enemies seeking to derail and distract you from your calling to step into leadership. The most formidable opponent you will face in your leadership journey is the man in the mirror. Winning the war within is how you conquer the resistance that is keeping you locked out of your promised land.

After examining my own life and speaking to thousands of men, I have identified the two prevailing mindsets that keep you stuck. I like to explain this with a visual of a road; when you're on this road, you are aligned with God's will for your life. You are progressing forward, thinking, acting, and feeling congruent with your convictions, calling, skill sets, and gift mix. You are KINGDOM DRIVEN.

Now, I want you to visualize a ditch on each side of this road. Both ditches come with LIES that seek to keep you questioning if you should even try to get out. These two ditches have become very comfortable and confusing to navigate.

DITCH 1: CHRISTIAN NICE GUY SYNDROME

This is where most Christian men live. The #1 trait of the 'Christian Nice Guy' is that he is PASSIVE instead of leading. Mr. Christian Nice Guy is always 'waiting' for someone to rescue him or for something to happen for him. This attitude and mindset is the result of incorrect beliefs we hold about God.

When you have this mindset, you say and believe things like: "If it's meant to be, it will happen," and "God is in control" …of everything despite your actions, decisions, and even your disobedience.

The two underlying beliefs of the Christian Nice Guy:

1. God will show up and rescue me and miraculously change my situation; no action necessary from me.

2. God will send someone to get me, a phone call, some mailbox money, or the crazy opportunity I could only dream of will fall in my lap.

The Christian Nice Guy lives with a victim mentality that has produced a passive man with a lottery mindset who does not lead in his life. This translates to the way he shows up as a husband, and father, and in his work. The Apostle Paul addresses this condition in his New Testament letter to the Corinthians. Corinthian Men are characterized by mediocrity, which leads to overextending grace, loose living, and casual Christianity.

DITCH 2: ORPHAN ALPHA SYNDROME

The Second Ditch is where most driven guys get stuck. There is a lot of energy expenditure in this ditch but not always a lot of movement, and if there is movement, you have to constantly question if you're heading in the right direction.

I call this mindset 'orphan alpha syndrome' because an orphan doesn't know their father and has no provider or protector. What results is a mindset of autonomous individualism, a self-generated willpower that will push doors open out of God's timing. An external alpha persona develops to protect internal insecurities and a scarcity mindset. These guys believe and recite the following mantras;

"If it's meant to be, it's up to me!" **and** ***"I am the captain of my soul and master of my fate."****

* This is a line from the well-known poem, Invictus written by William Ernest Henley, an avowed atheist, written in defiance to God.

This is the hustle and grind mindset rooted in 'the flesh,' which is what the Bible defines as our soul's willpower and natural energy operating apart from God. God does not accept work done from this mindset and REJECTS our self-driven effort. The Orphan Alpha is stuck in performance and is all about 'doing' with no 'being' or doing so he can feel accepted and valued. Don't mess up the order between being and doing, because doing something to try to be someone is the definition of religion, and it's a hard taskmaster.

THE CAIN CONDITION

There was a guy in the Bible who took a similar approach. His name was Cain. Cain brought an offering to the Lord from the best of what he could produce and got rejected. Have you ever wondered why God accepted Abel's offering but rejected Cain's? Cain's offering represented his best efforts and the results he could produce on his own and in his own natural strength.

It is a picture for us of what happens when you are driven to do your best, but your drive is not rooted in Christ, and you are the source. This is where most driven guys get tripped up: running in their own strength.

In the Bible, The Apostle Paul addresses this 'do the work' condition in his letter to the Galatians. Galatian men are characterized by striving, willpower, and self-dependence, which leads to legalism and performance-based living. This is false DOING.

The Christian Nice Guy (Corinthian man) and the Orphan Alpha (Galatian man) have counterfeit qualities of the man God designed them to be. Your human nature, apart from God, will show up like this:

- ☑ **YOU DEFAULT TO OLD PATTERNS OF LETHARGY AND MEDIOCRITY**
- ☑ **YOU PUSH YOURSELF TO PERFORM AND EXERCISE YOUR SELF-WILL IN EVERY SITUATION.**

Both of these expressions are rooted in 'self.'

WHERE ARE YOU RIGHT NOW?

Are you in Ditch 1 or Ditch 2? Maybe you're like me and have spent some time in both.

In the next chapter, I am going to share the most overlooked and misunderstood concept in the Bible.

IDENTIFYING THE RESISTANCE SUMMARY

Your belief system shapes the way you see and experience the world. Your beliefs have shaped your mindset, attitude and impact how you make your decisions in life.

Salvation is the door, not the destination. Making a commitment to follow Christ does not guarantee that you will reach the potential God has for your life. You must be intentional about your growth.

The greatest resistance to overcome is the internal war every man will face. The passive Christian Nice guy and the Orphan Alpha mindsets are at war with the Kingdom Driven Man that God has called you to be.

Ditch 1 is the "Christian Nice Guy Syndrome" mindset of passivity, victimhood, and a lottery/poverty mentality. The Christian Nice Guy is passive and waiting to be rescued. This attitude shows up in how he leads or does not lead in life.

Ditch 2 is the "Orphan Alpha Syndrome" mindset of hustling in your own strength, performance-driven living, independent from God with you as the source. The Orphan Alpha is under Adam's old curse of 'toil' aka 'hustle.' it's a paradigm of doing something in order to be someone.

Both mindsets are rooted in operating from "self" as source, rather than true identity as a son of God. If you don't understand God's pattern, purpose, or process, you will stay stuck in one of these ditches.

GET OUT OF THE GAP
TAKE RESPONSIBILITY

Up to this point, we've established God's original intent and goal for you. You are created for dominion, and there is a promised land for your life, a place where you operate with a GDV (God Driven Vision) and are functioning in your calling, anointing and gift mix. This place creates convergence, purpose, and fulfillment in your life.

We identified the external enemies that have set you up for failure and came face to face with the internal resistance that keeps you from stepping into leadership and cooperating with God in your life. The next step is the key to understanding how you shift from where you find yourself today and start closing the gap to be the man who's taking dominion in life.

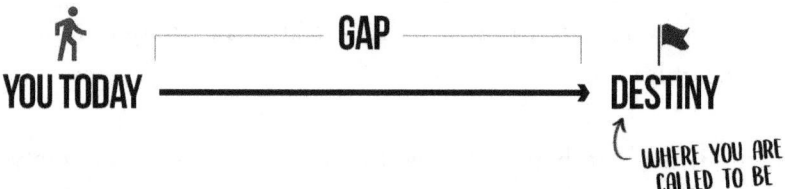

WHEN YOU'RE IN THE GAP, YOU ACT LIKE THIS:

- You seek pleasure
- You have a victim mindset
- You chase materialistic pursuits
- You never finish what you start
- You blame your wife for your marriage problems
- You blame shift everything; it's always someone else's fault
- You subscribe to limiting beliefs and substitute lies for truth

LET'S GET OUT OF THE GAP.

Remember 5th-grade science class where you learned the difference between Potential Energy vs. Kinetic Energy?

This is where you take a rock to the top of a hill (potential energy) vs. letting go of the rock, and all of the stored-up potential energy turns into momentum when a force is applied (aka kinetic energy). Applying force to an object with potential energy releases its potential.

Just because the object has potential DOES NOT translate to activating that potential. One of Scripture's biggest and most misunderstood secrets is the concept of potentiality.

Let's do further damage to the myth that once I get saved, I just sit back and let go and let God. Have you heard this before? I think it's a bumper sticker.

Not everything in the Bible is written directly to you, but it is written for you. The Bible is full of stories and warnings that explicitly demonstrate that reaching your full potential is NOT guaranteed. Here are a few examples of our Biblical heroes who never reached their full potential.

- Moses never made it to the Promised Land. Even though he accomplished many great things, he was disqualified from entering the land of Canaan.

- Samson took a Nazirite vow, which meant he was separated and consecrated to a holy lifestyle that honored God. However, he made some massive mistakes we can learn from, and he never fulfilled his vow.

- Solomon had a strong start and was gifted with supernatural wisdom from the Lord. However, by the end of his life, his many wives had turned him away from the Lord, and he built altars to strange gods.

These are examples that we are given to learn from so you are aware of the pitfalls that seek to derail your mission. You have the benefit of learning from others' mistakes.

So what's the lesson for us Ambitious Christian Business guys?

YOUR POTENTIAL DOES NOT GUARANTEE YOUR PROMISED LAND!

Having everything you need (POTENTIAL energy) is not the same as living in your identity and doing what you are called to do (KINETIC energy) to inherit your promised land and see your potential realized.

This first generation of Israelites took a 40-year detour through the wilderness from what was supposed to be an 11-day journey. They disqualified themselves from entering the Promised Land! They were still "SAVED" and "DELIVERED" from the bondage of Egypt. They experienced Passover under the blood and left their old life of slavery, but they

ALL DIED in the wilderness, except for two men, Joshua and Caleb. They could not get out of the GAP to the land they were given to occupy.

GOD FULFILLS HIS PROMISES, NOT YOUR POTENTIAL!

Only YOU can do that. This means that you are RESPONSIBLE for who you are and how you act. Everything you have and are experiencing right now in life is the result of your decisions. You are 100% responsible. Nothing will change unless you can take responsibility and own where you are in life right now.

So we are not sitting back on this journey and living in mediocrity like the passive Christian nice guy AND we are not striving to kick down all the doors in our own strength like an Orphan Alpha.

But, we see clearly that when God gives the direction and states His intention.

You must own it!

-If you don't like your marriage, STOP saying, *"If only I married the right person, if only she were different, if only she understood my needs..."* OWN IT!

-If you are frustrated with yourself and your circumstances, STOP saying, *"If only I were born into a better family... If only I had more money... If only I had what the other guy has..."* OWN IT!

-If you think everything and everyone is working against you...STOP thinking like a VICTIM and OWN IT!

God has given you a free agency that he highly respects and won't violate. You have the power of choice. Whatever you are not changing, you are choosing. Here's the good news: you don't control everything, but you control some things. Think of your potential like this equation:

PREPARATION + OPPORTUNITY = PROMOTION

There is a controllable and an uncontrollable here. You can't do God's job, but you can control the controllable.

YOUR DECISIONS DETERMINE YOUR DESTINY

God esteems your free will so highly that He won't touch it. The implication of this is that you are the result of your decisions. This applied to Adam, and it still applies to you. One of the biggest flaws in our Christian thinking is that the results I have in life are based on the cards I have been dealt; *"everything is a result of God's will for my life."*

My favorite misquoted verse is Romans 8:28 which says *"And we know that God causes all things to work together for good to those who love God, to those who are called according to His purpose"*

Many use this verse as a blanket statement that everything in your life is always working for your good. But you can't have verse 28 without verse 29:

"For those whom He foreknew, He also predestined to become conformed to the image of His Son,"

The key is that God can and will use everything that happens in your life, regardless of your mistakes and missteps, for your benefit IF you are active in participating in His process of being conformed. Part of being a son is responsibility. Sons are led by God. This is not passive. Sons listen and take obedient action.

Low-level thinking removes all responsibility from your life and claims that if you are not overcoming, "it's not your fault." This is victim thinking, blame-shifting, and complaining. Everything that happens to you in life may not be your fault, but it is your responsibility.

YOU ARE 100% RESPONSIBLE

Having potential does not guarantee results. Potential is released through responsibility, commitment, and action. In the next chapter, we will look at the most common ways men try to pursue their potential and why these avenues don't work and leave you frustrated.

GET OUT OF THE GAP SUMMARY

Potential alone does not guarantee your success. Achieving your destiny requires active participation through daily decisions and your commitment to growth. You have the power of choice.

You must take full responsibility for every choice you make in life. You are the result of your decisions. Everything you experience may not be your fault, but it is your responsibility.

Taking ownership means acknowledging your present circumstances instead of blame-shifting. Make a commitment to control what is in your power and take responsibility for where you are today.

THE WAY FORWARD
RETHINKING THE WAY WE HAVE ALWAYS DONE IT

So when it comes to rebuilding ourselves, becoming the man God can use, what do we do? What tools or resources are available for Christian guys like us?

1. DO NOTHING.

This story is sadly too familiar. Most men will do nothing. They will suffer in silence, grit their teeth, bear the pressure, and bury the pain. They carry the hurt of a broken marriage or the internal struggle over past events and trauma they endured or caused.

But "doing nothing" is rarely ever actually "doing nothing." Everyone needs an outlet. So, if this is you, you will find a coping mechanism, a medication to escape the reality you feel trapped in and that you also created. I call this vicious cycle PMS.

THE PMS CYCLE

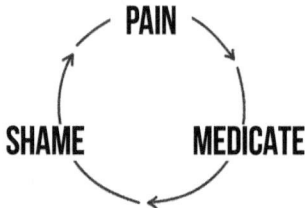

PAIN - MEDICATE - SHAME
Trigger- feel pain- medicate- feel shame

Self-medication can take the form of alcohol, porn, work, food, and even fitness to mask what's really going on underneath your armor. When you are stuck in PMS, you wear a mask to show the world you're OK or cover up your struggle with being "busy." Work more, eat more, go to the gym more. You will do anything to get numb and escape the pain you feel.

2. PASSIVE CHRISTIANITY.

This mindset believes in God's power to intervene and miraculously change a situation supernaturally. I believe in the power of God and have experienced it in my life. The passive man is waiting for God to rescue him and miraculously change his character and his habits and supernaturally fast forward his spiritual growth. If you believe this, you will be stuck waiting.

There is not one example in the Bible where Jesus ever changed a man's character or gave him new habits. After a miracle or supernatural intervention, He always tells them what to do. At this point, God will walk that man through a process to become the man He has destined him to be.

Transformation, aka 'Spiritual growth,' never happens by accident.

3. WILLPOWER.

Driven men have been exercising their willpower for ages in an effort to change their situation. Self-effort can sustain some transformation for a while… until it can't. The willpower to change your behavior and try hard will always result in burnout and end with you hitting a wall. This is because science now shows us that willpower is a limited resource. You don't have an endless supply. Trying hard is commendable but is not sustainable.

4. MEN'S BIBLE STUDY.

The only other option for Christian guys has been a traditional Men's group. This can take the form of a weekly or monthly Bible study, a men's breakfast, or maybe a men's group branded with a name on-trend. I love the church and the effort put forth by these groups. Heck, some churches have NOTHING to offer men! But when you peel back the curtain on most men's gatherings, they end up being book clubs. In others, you watch a video and then circle up for some superficial conversation. Most of these guys have been struggling on repeat with the same issues and have become very skilled with keeping their masks on and never letting others see what's really going on.

At the end of the day, the volunteer hosting this meeting was tapped to lead the conversation by the leadership and isn't up to the task of dealing with the modern-day pressures, past traumas, and present challenges you're dealing with. I am all in for fellowship and fun, but BBQ, UFC, and talking about the game doesn't facilitate the true transformation you need.

Even deep Bible study won't bring the transformation you require. The early church walked in power and was largely illiterate, with no physical Bibles like the ones you and I have so readily available today. Studying the Bible, memorizing scripture, or getting a degree in biblical studies never leads to transformation because 'thinking' alone doesn't change you.

5. COACHING GROUPS.

I believe in coaching, and I believe everyone needs a coach. The challenge in the personal development world of coaching is that most programs don't share the values of the Kingdom of God. These 'programs,' even though some may be run by those professing to be Christians, are full of danger zones for us as followers of Christ. The most common scenarios I see are:

- Motivational coaching with mystical and new age manifestation elements
- Men's coaching programs full of vulgarity and compromise
- The rise and grind build 'your empire' mindset
- A hyperfocus on prosperity with no grid for obedience, suffering and conformity to Christ in your character and conduct

These programs leave you in a place where you have to eat the meat and spit out a lot of bones.

WARNING: If you pursue coaching from outlets that don't operate in alignment with the Kingdom of God, you may be putting yourself at risk. The Kingdom principle states that fruit reproduces after its own kind. So, you will see the values and worldview of the coach, guru, or influencer you're following show up in your attitude and life.

In Luke 8:18, Jesus instructs us to pay attention to what we hear. We are living in a culture that is voraciously consuming content; we are inundated with voices competing for our attention. It is imperative that you guard your gates and watch what you allow to enter your domain. My modern-day application of Luke 8:18 sounds like this, "don't subscribe to every voice in your feed."

Are you ready to make this as simple as possible? You need to understand the system, principles, and government that God operates with. The problem we need to overcome right now is how you, as a Christian man, can regain dominion over all areas of your life. Most men will resort to hard work or guess work when they really need a framework. In the next chapter, I'll show you the Kingdom Driven Order and give you the framework to build your life on the right foundation so you can release your potential and fulfill your dominion mandate.

THE WAY FORWARD SUMMARY

The old ways men have used to encounter transformation don't work. The most common approaches are outlined below.

Do Nothing: Most men will do nothing and get stuck in the vicious cycle of PMS. PMS starts with a trigger that causes pain. This trigger causes you to seek a form of self-medication like alcohol, drugs, food, or porn. As a result, you feel ashamed of your behavior. It's the pain-medicate-shame cycle.

Passive Christianity: Passive Christian nice guys are waiting on God to impart new habits and character development. You will be stuck waiting if this is you because God doesn't operate this way.

Willpower is a limited resource, and men who solely rely on their will eventually hit a wall because the approach of white-knuckling behavior change is not sustainable.

Traditional Bible Study and men's groups are well-intentioned. Many are under-equipped to facilitate true transformation, which takes intensive focus with intention in an environment of committed men.

Traditional coaching programs are full of pitfalls that Kingdom Driven Men must avoid, like new age practices, vulgarity, compromise, and the build your empire mindset that doesn't account for the values of God's Kingdom.

Be careful who you follow. Influencers and coaching programs that are not based on Kingdom truth with maturity can reproduce their worldview in your mindset and attitude.

PART III:
KINGDOM DRIVEN ORDER

MOVING FROM CHAOS TO ORDER
INTRODUCING THE KINGDOM DRIVEN ORDER

Are you ready to move out of the chaos in Ditch 1, Ditch 2, or from one-dimensional success and align your whole life in order with God's Kingdom? You can be the man God created you to be; it doesn't have to be elusive or confusing. But you need to understand your spiritual anatomy.

You are created in God's image as a triune being with three parts. You are a spirit, you have a soul, and you live in a body. When you come to Christ, you become a new creation. Your spirit, the eternal part of you that, as a result of sin, is dead, receives divine life. At this point, you receive a spiritual seed that is downloaded into your new DNA. The seed contains all of the information you need for growth- it's the blueprint. God's goal is that you will grow and mature according to the potential within the seed.

THE BATTLE

When you are born again, you are born into battle. In part I, we covered the external enemies and the war within that must be won. But what is this battle over? The enemy's goal is to stop your growth at all costs. His strategy is to keep you the same man as you are right now—no growth, living a life of unmet potential.

Modern-day Christianity has the salvation message down. You received preaching about how God forgives your sins… but you never got the second part. This is why many men are saved and stuck.

If you are only told Jesus died for your sins and it stops there, you are missing the tools to align and walk out the Christian life. I stated earlier that without the proper instruction, you may never experience the growth that God intends for you so you can reach your full potential.

Too many men are frustrated and wandering through their wilderness in life, wanting to get to the promised land. It doesn't have to be this way. You were never given the map or the tools to fully unlock the unmet potential residing within the seed.

How does growth occur? One word:

TRANSFORMATION

Transformation is a process that God uses to make you THE MAN.

THE MAN God created you to be
THE MAN your family is waiting for
THE MAN your world is waiting for
THE MAN that God can trust to promote you to the next level.

My GDV (God Driven Vision) and mission is to help ambitious Christian men like you get vision and clarity and then relentlessly execute that mission. Because I believe the world is waiting for you to SHOW UP POWERFULLY!

God is not a respecter of persons; He respects principles. Transformation does not occur through information, willpower, or motivation. You need a framework and you need Kingdom principles with practice to reach His goal for your life.

In the first chapter of Genesis, we observe:

"The earth was formless and void, and darkness was over the surface of the deep…"

Genesis 1:2

The world was in desolation and a chaotic condition. Then God speaks:

"LET THERE BE LIGHT"

Over the next five consecutive days, God will continue to speak, create, and bring order to what was once chaotic. On the sixth day, man is created and inherits something he never had to work for.

When God creates and invades an atmosphere, He brings order. The Bible is a record of God bringing order to the chaos within man after sin entered the world with the final solution being fully embodied in Jesus.

What if I told you there's a blueprint for spiritual and practical dominion hidden in plain sight in Scripture? I discovered a pattern in scripture and started implementing this order within my life. It is responsible for moving my life from the painful problems and chaotic state you may find yourself in today and transforming it into order. Since testing and proving this in my own life, I started implementing it with the men I work with inside the Standard 59 Mastermind.

Discover the transformative power of the Kingdom Driven Order, where biblical wisdom meets modern science. Installing this order will upgrade your operating system so you can dominate in life. We'll devote entire chapters to each element of the Kingdom Driven Order in the pages that follow. I will tell you what it is and why it works and give you an example of how to implement it.

ALIGN
Build an Unshakable Identity

DESIGN
Take Dominion Over Your Day

WEAPONIZE
Access Your Authority For Impact and Influence

OPTIMIZE
Master Your Mind and Strengthen Your Spirit

DOMINION

ALIGN
BUILD AN UNSHAKABLE IDENTITY

Understanding your identity is the first and most important step in unlocking your purpose and potential in alignment with God's process. When we examine the strategy of the enemy, it is always connected to an attack on who you are—your identity in Christ. All of the attacks from the external enemies you face are directly opposed to you understanding and aligning with your God-given identity.

Your belief system is the foundation of your life. What you believe dictates what you think, feel, and do. The first belief we must install is a correct view of God. How you see God will shape the way you see yourself and your world.

If you received a passed-down religious image of a judge with a gavel who is full of demands, impossible to please, and waiting for you to mess up so he can teach you a lesson, then your identity will be shaped by this belief.

If you replace the religious image of a distant, demanding God with a Father who loves, guards, protects, and provides for His children, then you see yourself differently. This view will impact the thoughts you think, how you feel, and how you act.

The war is raging over WHO you are and what you believe about yourself, which impacts HOW you see yourself. Let's take a multiple-choice quiz right now. What lens have you been seeing yourself through?

A. I am a sinner saved by grace.

B. I am a son who has been redeemed and regenerated, and I now live from a new source of supernatural power to be who God says I am and to execute my mission with His authority.

If you ONLY find your identity as a saved sinner, you will never fully operate in your mission with clarity, purpose, and power. Men who only live in a conscious awareness of their sin can never move into the power available to them. Inside the Standard 59 Mastermind, we train to be Christ-conscious over being sin-conscious. Behavior modification techniques and habit stacking in order to be someone doesn't work in God's Kingdom.

The first step in the Kingdom Driven Order is to ALIGN with your identity as a son. I am not here to give you a new identity. I am reminding you of who you really are. Being a son is something we have lost in modern Christianity. We are programmed to work for God and perform to gain His approval, but working for God can never compare to walking with God. This internal performance programming is installed at a young age regardless of your faith upbringing.

As men, we evaluate ourselves and others based on what I call the BIG THREE LIES society tells us, and we believe.

LIE #1: You are what you do.

LIE #2: You are what you have.

LIE #3: You are what others say about you.

This is where most men get their identity and value.

Satan is strategic. Jesus warns us that he roams like a lion, seeking those he can devour. The enemy is a keen observer of our behavior and weaknesses, and he is patiently waiting for the right opportunity to launch his attack. The primary attack in his playbook is attacking your identity. If he can separate you from the family and isolate you, he has successfully sidelined your potential to inflict damage on the kingdom of darkness, and you are guaranteed to miss your inheritance. Just like Esau, you will end up trading what rightfully belongs to you for something that gives you instant gratification. Esau forfeited his birthright and inheritance for a bowl of stew. You can read the full story in Genesis 25.

Your identity is under attack. The same attack satan launches at you is what he deployed against Jesus. What is the primary question when satan visits Jesus in the wilderness?

ARE YOU REALLY A SON?

Immediately after Jesus is baptized in the Jordan and the Father declares, "This is my beloved son in whom I am well pleased." Jesus heads straight into the wilderness for 40 days before launching His public ministry. During this time, satan will appear and tempt Him three times. With each offer that is made to Jesus, the temptation is always prefaced with this statement: *"If you really are the Son of God..."*

His identity was under attack. Like Jesus, the enemy will also question and attack your status as a son. We must be grounded in full knowledge, security, and confidence of who we are and whose we are. The identity of all Kingdom Driven Men is rooted in knowing God as our Father. We are sons of God! A son isn't confused or suffering from an identity crisis. The foundation for EVERY man must be grounded in the foundation of being a son. Sons have nothing to fear, nothing to prove, nothing to lose, and nothing to hide.

The main barrier to understanding and operating like a son is the orphan mindset. An orphan mindset manifests as limiting beliefs that cause you to see yourself as a victim and operate from insecurity and uncertainty. King Saul in the Bible was appointed King, but operated like an orphan, and it disqualified him from ruling.

SAUL SYNDROME

King Saul is tall, strong, and charismatic. People are naturally drawn to his outward appearance and the way he handles himself. He is a leader who inspires others to greatness. The Prophet Samuel anoints him to be king. Based on all of this, Saul should be secure in his leadership, but he does not see himself as King, and his behavior follows that of an orphan. He's jealous, insecure, lacks integrity, is disobedient, and full of fear. Instead of using his authority as king, he uses power to manipulate and control. Saul becomes proud, rebellious and acts independent of God, rejecting His authority and instruction.

The orphan mindset in Saul manifested as insecurity and affected his self-image. The Bible states that Saul saw himself as "little in his own eyes"(1 Sam 15:16)." This insecurity moved to independence, which showed up as pride. He suffered from what others thought of him, known as the fear of man (Proverbs 29:25), which resulted in disobedience and disqualified him from being king. The orphan mindset keeps men trapped in insecurity. When you are insecure, it can manifest in victim beliefs or independence, rebellion, and pride.

We are all born slaves to sin and inherit the fallen nature of Adam. Many men have made a commitment to Christ and are saved but still live like orphans, unaware of their sonship. When you follow Jesus, He replaces the spirit of slavery with the spirit of adoption. Jesus tells His disciples, "I will not leave you as orphans, I will come to you" (John 14:8). The Lord has predestined you to be adopted as a son. You can not operate as an orphan and embrace your sonship at the same time.

Have you ever noticed that when a man is introduced for the first time in the Bible, we are given their genealogy?

- Joseph is the son of Jacob
- Joshua is the son of Nun
- David is the son of Jesse

In the Hebrew culture, men were identified by their sonship, not their occupation. The lesson is that we operate as sons of God on earth. Our

BEING in sonship is where we find our identity. God is more concerned with who you are than what you do.
If you're focused on high performance and doing first, you're operating in the wrong order.

- Performance in business
- Performance in life
- Performance with God

Just because The Father sees you as a son doesn't mean you don't get stuck in these cycles of striving, performance-based living followed by defeat, depression, and despair.

You have to BE…. then you have to DO

BEING: Who you are
DOING: What you do because of who you are

Joshua: The Lord instructs Joshua to BE strong and BE courageous, then he will DO and have success. Joshua 1:8

Daniel: The Lord tells Daniel that people who KNOW their God will BE strong and take action. Daniel 11:32

Jesus: When Jesus delivers the sermon on the Mount, he speaks of being and doing. "Those who hunger and thirst for righteousness shall BE satisfied."

"Therefore everyone who hears these words of Mine and acts on them, may be compared to a wise man who built his house on the rock."
Matthew 7:24

It's always "Be," then "Do" in God's Kingdom

STEP 1. BEING- *WHO you are: You are a new creation species.*

STEP 2. DOING- *WHAT you DO because of WHO you are. You are created for good works.*

Everything we do flows out of who we are, and that starts with how you see yourself.

There are many words throughout the Bible that explain our relationship with God.

The Lord's servants: Carry delegated responsibility
Bond slaves: Carry responsibilities out of love and devotion to the master
Ministers: Have people entrusted to them
Stewards: Have resources to manage and multiply
Workers: Have actions to take and a job to complete

Above all of the roles you fill, the work you accomplish, and the titles you carry:

YOU ARE A SON

Your underlying belief system will determine your identity.

Your behavior will always follow your identity.

Every decision you make is based on your identity and built on your beliefs. As sons of God in the Kingdom, we order our behavior in alignment with how God sees us. We believe and act in accordance with what we think is true. To fulfill our potential, we need to be trained on how sons act and align our actions in a manner worthy of our calling.

The latest psychological research demonstrates that the fastest way to build or break a habit is to take on a new identity. Neuroscience bears out that 'trying' through willpower to change a behavior or build a habit is almost useless without changing your identity.

- If you want a physical transformation you need to take on the identity of an athlete.
- If you enlist in battle, you must see yourself as a warrior equipped for the fight.
- If you are a son of God, you must operate as a son.

Your behavior will follow the identity you install.

THIS IS WHO I AM. THIS IS WHAT I DO.

As Kingdom Driven Men we have an unfair advantage. You have access to the Holy Spirit who functions within you as a power source to energize your life and decisions.

In the next chapter, we will explore how deliberately structuring our time in accordance with our divine design unleashes your full potential.

ALIGN SUMMARY

Understanding your identity is the first and most important step in unlocking your purpose and potential in alignment with God's process.

Your belief system is the foundation of your life. What you believe dictates what you think, feel, and do. Your internal beliefs in alignment with how you see yourself will dictate and impact every decision you make in life.

How you view God will shape your identity, self-value, and the value you assign to others. It is imperative to understand that God is your Father, and you are a son.

The enemy will always attack your identity in Christ; his strategy is to test and question if you see yourself as a son and know your God-given authority.

The main barrier to operating like a son is the orphan mindset. An orphan mindset manifests as limiting beliefs that cause you to either operate from insecurity and uncertainty or independence and pride.

A Kingdom Driven man's core identity comes from being a son of God, not from performance, occupation, gifts, abilities, or what others say.

Behavior always follows identity. In the Kingdom, it's BE and then DO. "This is who I am. This is what I do."

DESIGN
TAKE DOMINION OVER YOUR DAY

The #1 fallacy is that you believe you have more time than you actually do. How many times have you said, 'Someday,' I will get in shape 'someday,' I will go for the promotion 'someday,' I will start the business 'someday,' I will write the book 'someday. 'Someday' is not a day of the week. Will you keep telling yourself "one day I will start." Or instead of saying one day, will you commit to day one?

How many dreams have been delayed because someone kept waiting for someday? Your days are numbered. We are good at thinking we have more time or contemplating life from a future lens while bypassing the present moments.

How do you measure the quality of your life? By measuring the quality of your day. If you want to take dominion in life, you must take dominion over your day. Failure to master your day is failure to master your life. Your goal is to take dominion over your life, which starts with taking dominion over your day. Here's the truth:

The way you're living today is the way you're living your life.

Let's revisit our Dominion Mandate. God gave you five commands. Let's reframe these as personal questions to develop a baseline and become aware of where you are.

- **BEAR FRUIT:** Where am I producing specific and measurable results in my life?
- **MULTIPLY:** What is multiplying in my life right now?
- **REPLENISH:** Am I refilling and fueling myself?
- **SUBDUE:** What resistance am I overcoming in my life right now?
- **TAKE DOMINION:** Where am I dominating in my life right now?

These commands are also Kingdom principles. The fact is, you are bearing fruit in your life right now. The question is, what is the quality of the fruit you are producing? You can produce the fruit of the Spirit, like love, peace, and joy, or based on what you are sowing, you may instead be reaping anger, unrest, and frustration.

All men multiply. The question is, what is multiplying in your life right now?

You are created to subdue and take dominion, but the present-day condition of most men is rushed, reactive, and distracted. Instead of designing your life, you get caught in a vicious cycle of life happening to you. This chaos pushes you into a survival mode mentality. When you are inconsistent and casual in your approach to life, you will always feel like you are running behind and can never catch up. Being casual creates casualties. You must operate out of your identity as a son of God with a clear vision of who you are and where you are going.

God's goal for you is that you would operate from a powerful state of being with energy to dominate your day. Your state of being is how you think, feel, and act. It's your present experience moment by moment. The commands to 'be strong' and 'be courageous' are commands connected to your state of being. Thinking empowering thoughts create powerful feelings that result in taking bold action.

YOUR FOCUS IS UNDER ATTACK

To operate at this level will require your full focus. Your focus produces energy. The enemy knows that when you are focused, you are powerful, so he works to divide your attention and fracture your focus. His strategy is crafted to hijack your state of being and to make you think, feel, and act out of alignment with your true identity. He uses technology through the present-day media machine to engineer distractions that rewire your brain's neural pathways and your ability to focus and retain attention.

The battle is over what you believe. Television became popular in the 1950s. Soon, every home had one, which became the medium for getting the news and receiving "programming." As technology advances, we find ourselves in the 24-hour news cycle and social media feeds designed for infinite scrolling. There is literally no end to the scroll. That's why it's called doom-scrolling. This media is designed to keep you reactive. When you constantly receive different messages from different sources, you build new neural pathways in your brain that keep you hunting for new stimuli and trigger reactive emotions within you. The system has been created to condition you to be a reactive consumer. Entertainment is anesthesia; when you are constantly consuming, you cannot be creating.

With unlimited access to 'free' social media, you become the product. Your attention is now monetized. The average adult in the U.S. checks their phone 352 times a day, that's about once every three minutes. The source driving this addiction is dopamine. Dopamine is a feel-good chemical responsible for drive, motivation, and the anticipation of a reward. Anticipation of a reward drives addiction to technology, porn, food and the list goes on. That's what dopamine does.

Large corporations that control and own the media know this and employ behavior psychologists to design apps that keep you on them for as long as possible because you are the product. The ads you receive through this medium are designed to change the way you think, feel, and act, influencing your state of being. To dominate your day, you must be equipped to turn off the dopamine drip.

Besides the rewiring of your brain, other harmful effects of spending too much time on social media are:

- Comparison and envy
- Low self-esteem
- Addiction and Isolation

When we are not tethered to technology, we are immersed in the hustle-hard culture. "Rise and grind" has become the badge of honor for the most successful social media influencers and entrepreneurs. As men, we have internal wiring to work, produce, and create. So, the trap of hustling harder is always before us. But hustling hard and rising to grind is opposed to our position as sons of God. The curse that sin brought into the earth was for man to work with hard labor and toil to see results. Living from this mentality is the modern-day hustle-hard culture.

Sons operate from rest. This means doing less, not more. Men in the first century had their own competing priorities and responsibilities. Jesus instructed them and you to:

"Come to Me, all who are weary and heavy-laden, and I will give you rest. Take My yoke upon you and learn from Me, for I am gentle and humble in heart, and YOU WILL FIND REST FOR YOUR SOULS. For My yoke is easy and My burden is light."

Matthew 11:28-30

There is a secret in scripture that is a game changer for how you operate on the daily, do the right things, and get more done. Let's see what we can learn from the life of David.

BEFORE he ascended to the throne as king,
BEFORE he was promoted from the pastures to the palace,
BEFORE he was entrusted with a nation,

He could be found in a grassy pasture doing ordinary work and praying this while he was on the job:

"ONE THING have I desired from the LORD: that I shall seek: "That I may dwell in the house of the LORD all the days of my life, To behold the beauty of the LORD and meditate in His temple."

Psalm 27:4

This ONE habit, done daily, guided the shepherd in his transformation to king. David was a man of priorities; it wasn't about doing all the things. He focused on ONE THING, and everything fell into order and alignment when he did.

Investing time with the Lord every morning is a cornerstone habit in the life of every man of God who ascended in influence and made an impact. David calls this "awakening the dawn." Joseph practiced this habit while in a pit, and it guided him to 2nd in command over the nation of Egypt. Daniel practiced this three times a day, leading to his promotion in Babylon. Jesus is the most effective and efficient man that ever lived, and He can be found before sunrise in a 'certain' place in prayer with His Father.

When you understand God's ways are not your ways, you will start to realize that God doesn't do it the same way the world has programmed you to operate. Socrates and Aristotle have influenced the way we think more than God's word has. You have been programmed by Western logic, which causes you to overthink everything. But the wisdom of the world is "bass-awkward" with how God does things.

God's ways will always be viewed as COUNTERINTUITIVE to what we think with our natural minds.

The first shall be last, and the last shall be first. Those who learn to wait, go the farthest, and Jesus can be found in a holding pattern, waiting for His Father's timing. When you're an ambitious business guy with a full agenda, you want to run right out of the gates, maximize productivity, and G.S.D. (get 'stuff' done) everything on your punch list. It's counterintuitive to pause and pray. There is a practice I help men implement to build this habit, and it's found in the life of Moses.

Moses was a high-level business leader responsible for governing the nation of Israel. He was pressed for time, and the demands of leadership kept his schedule full. Before the Tabernacle was built, God met with Moses in a tent about half a mile from his home office. This is known in scripture as:

THE TENT OF MEETING

The Tent of Meeting is where you start your day with God. Sons operate from rest. One of our non-negotiables inside the Standard 59 Mastermind is having a Tent of Meeting installed into your morning routine. The tent of meeting signifies meeting with God in a certain place and at a certain time.

We use a protocol called Rise and Rest. This stands in direct contradiction to the rise-and-grind wisdom of the world because you accelerate more by resting in your tent. Scripture records that Jesus had a habit of going to a "certain place" to pray. David refers to this as the "secret place" in Psalm 91, and Jesus instructs us in Matthew 6:6 that when we pray, we should enter our prayer closet and shut the door. Because of this constant communion with His Father, He gets more done in less time.

In John 15:5 Jesus states *"I am the vine, you are the branches. He who abides in Me, and I in him, bears much fruit; for without Me you can do nothing."* Jesus is teaching that being fruitful and having results in life is directly determined by the quantity and quality of time invested in your tent of meeting.

It's common for men to think they don't have enough time to pray. This natural mindset is focused on productivity by constantly 'doing.' When you live with a consistent fast pace in your life, you will find it challenging at first to slow down to pause and build a prayer habit. The secret every man of God knows in scripture is that prayer never wastes time. Prayer qualifies you for promotion. Joshua was chosen as Moses' successor. The secret to his promotion can be found in Exodus 33:11. Moses had just met with God in the tent of meeting, and then we read, *"When Moses returned to the camp, his servant Joshua, the son of Nun, a young man, would not depart from the tent."* Joshua prioritized being in the presence of the Lord, which led to his promotion.

Nothing produces a more powerful state of being than meeting with God and entering His presence in your tent of meeting. When you do this consistently, you prime yourself to enter a flow state, which is defined as a state where you are focused, full of energy, and completely in tune with the task at hand.

Even though the word flow wasn't coined until recently, we can witness men in scripture operating in flow. When Joshua leads the march around the walls of Jericho, when David is aiming his sling at Goliath's head, and when Jesus is in early morning prayer fellowshipping with His Father, you see states of flow. James describes the prayer of faith as effective, fervent, and focused; this is flow.

Designing your day and developing focus means you must disable distractions. The Apostle Paul instructs his mentee Timothy to divorce himself from distractions (2 Timothy 2:4). Building this level of focus starts in our tent of meeting and influences everything we do. Disabling distractions means saying yes to the thing that we are focusing on and saying no to opportunities that derail our focus. Say yes, and then rigorously defend your yes with no's.

Once you align with your identity as a son, you take the right actions based on this identity. When you consistently command your behavior, you build habits that form and solidify your character, which will determine your destiny.

The word 'habit' is missing from most modern Bible translations, but the concept of habit-building is obvious; when Jesus gives a command, it is inherent in the text that it is to be done habitually. Greek scholar Kenneth Wuest, author of the Wuest translation, brings the concept of following Jesus' commands as repeated habitual actions to life. Jesus knew your daily actions become your habits, and your habits become your character.

"Therefore, everyone who is of such a character as to be habitually hearing these words of mine and habitually doing them, shall be likened to an intelligent man who is of such a nature that he built his house upon the rocky cliff."

Matthew 7:24
Wuest Translation

> **ACTIONS > HABITS > CHARACTER > DESTINY**

LIFE IS SHORT

Scripture reminds us that life is shorter than we think.

"Yet you do not know what your life will be like tomorrow. You are just a vapor that appears for a little while and then vanishes away."
James 4:14

"For we will certainly die and are like water that is spilled on the ground and cannot be gathered up again…"
2 Samuel 14:14

One of my mentors shocked me with a statement he made during a message I was listening to where he stated:

"Every time I am present during our assembly times, I am very conscious that this may be the last time I'll ever speak.

So, what you heard today was because I was being prepared, not really knowing for sure that there would be another day after today. When I think about today, I want to make sure that I am able to communicate and impart everything that the Lord has placed in me.

"I am really living on the edge of eternity all the time. That's where I live. I have no desire to live another day apart from seeing the will of God realized."

-Doug Riggs

Months later, Doug graduated from this life. His words still resonate in my spirit, "Do you live with the edge of eternity in view? If you were told today would be your last day on planet Earth, would you live differently?" I am using Doug's statements as fuel for following God's call on my life and living each day to make the most impact that I can. Because your days are numbered, you must learn to steward your time and dominate your day so you can take dominion for the Kingdom.

I have downloaded an app called 'Life,' which visually displays how many years you have lived and how many years you have left based on some inputs. It is striking to see how many months and years you have left on planet Earth and it serves as a reminder to make each day count and live it as if it could be your last day. Below you can see a visual representation of your life in months. Find your age on the chart and reflect on where you are today and how much time you have left. Do you have a plan to unlock the God Given potential you are carrying?

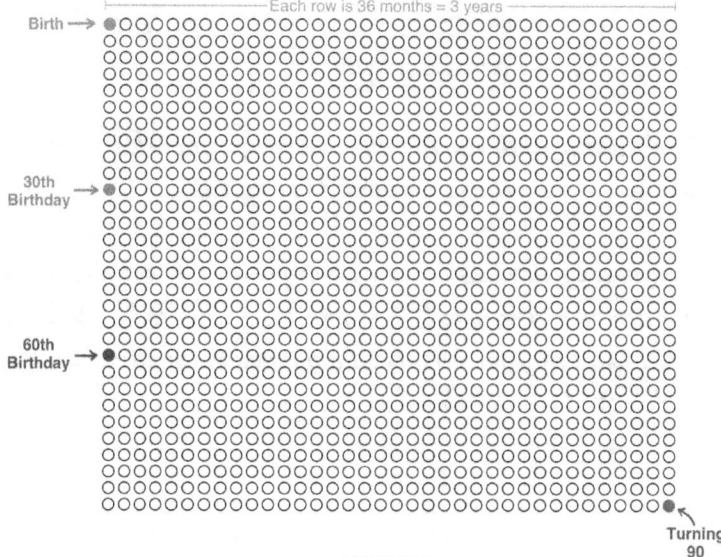

DESIGN SUMMARY

The way you live today is the way you are living your life. Designing your days through intention and structure is essential for dominating your life and fulfilling your potential.

You must train yourself to operate from a powerful state of being with energy to dominate your day. Your state of being is how you think, feel, and act. It's your present experience moment by moment.

Your focus is under attack. The enemy knows that when you are focused, you are powerful, so he works to divide your attention and fracture your focus. Distractions break your focus and influence your state of being. Rule or be ruled.

The Tent of Meeting is where you start your day with God and align your identity. Jesus states and models that we get more done when we abide in Him. Investing time in your tent of meeting builds your focus and primes you to navigate each day effectively.

Habit building is biblical, and the commands and teachings of Jesus are to be practiced habitually. Your daily actions become habits that shape your character and determine your destiny.

WEAPONIZE
THE WARRIOR'S MINDSET

God placed man in the Garden of Eden and told him to cultivate it and keep it. The phrase to keep it is more accurately translated as to guard it. Adam was to be a watchman, observing, preserving, and protecting. There is an enemy implied in this command given to man. Adam is charged with defending what God has given him authority over by guarding against all enemy intrusion.

Your role as a man is to be a strong protector, keeper, and watchman over the work the Lord has entrusted you with. Adam failed this test when he sat by passively while the serpent engaged Eve in a deceptive dialogue. Adam was present the entire time. Instead of watching over the Garden, he watched as his wife disobeyed, and then he blindly followed along.

Ever since the intrusion in the Garden, this world has been under attack from God's enemy, also known as the adversary. The result of this cosmic war between the kingdom of darkness and the Kingdom of Light is the world's fallen and broken condition. When you become a Christian and make a commitment to King Jesus you are enrolling in an army. Men struggle in life and are defeated because they never understood they were born into a war and are fighting a real enemy. They run through cycles of defeat with the same battles because they have not been equipped with the knowledge of how to weaponize.

The Bible warns us not to be ignorant of the devil and his schemes. The enemy's strategy is to take advantage of every failure you make to break into your life and cause your downfall. Being a mature son in the Kingdom comes with responsibility. Paul instructs Timothy to fight the good fight of faith. This could also be understood as the warfare of faith. This is more than a shallow subscription to a superficial Christianity. To exercise sonship is to attain the goal for which you have been saved.

In the Old Testament, the goal for the Nation of Israel was to attain and possess the land of Canaan, their promised land. The goal of your sonship is to attain the full stature and development God desires you to walk in. This is known as your inheritance. Paul referred to this attaining in his life as the "upward" call in Philippians 3:14.

"I press on toward the goal for the prize of the upward call of God in Christ Jesus."

The means of attaining our full and complete destiny will come through warfare. When the nation of Israel sent spies into the Promised Land, the report that was returned stated there were giants in the land. These enemy occupiers were illegally squatting on the real estate that God had given to Israel, and Israel must dispossess their enemies before possession can take place. You are not fighting people or physical giants in your quest to fulfill your call, but you are immersed in a battle against spiritual forces and powers that will oppose every step you make to take your territory.

The Apostle Paul provides powerful metaphors that illustrate the battle we are born into and the intensity of the warfare surrounding our inheritance. He paints a vivid picture for his first-century audience against the backdrop of the Roman games with images that would have carried deep meaning to his hearers. When Paul states that we are wrestling against rulers, powers, and principalities of the darkness of this age, the struggle he is depicting is the Roman wrestling matches of the first century. These were bloody battles in close quarters with hand-to-hand combat.

Paul's solution is the command to armor up. When God calls you, He equips you. Your part in the battle is to learn how to get in the fight in partnership with God. How do you fight? You weaponize. This is why the next element within the Kingdom Driven Order is to weaponize by learning to walk in and access your God-given authority. The first way we weaponize is by taking on a new mindset. The Apostle Paul mentors Timothy into this new way of thinking in the following verse:

"No soldier in active service entangles himself in the affairs of everyday life, so that he may please the one who enlisted him as a soldier."

2 Timothy 2:4

Most men live like civilians when they are called to be soldiers. These are two opposing mindsets. Civilians in normal society walk around oblivious to the role of warriors. They can easily become careless consumers preoccupied with pleasing themselves, entangled in everyday affairs and civilian pursuits. The apostle contrasts the civilian lifestyle and attitude with that of a soldier enlisted in active service. The soldier does not live for himself but chooses to live to please his enlisting officer.

THE CIVILIAN MINDSET

Civilians live for themselves. The default operating system is to live a life that operates from their desires. These desires aren't necessarily sinful but natural and made apart from God. Civilian decisions are governed by what they want and when they want it. The 'self-life' is on the throne in the heart of this casual Christian.

THE WARRIOR MINDSET

Warriors are disciplined. A soldier's operating system is to view himself as enlisted in an army with an assignment. Personal appetites and low-level cravings are set aside for the mission. Warriors are governed by a code to please the one who enlisted them. Warriors filter all decisions by serving the objective for which they have been called.

To be a warrior is to seek first the Kingdom of God and His righteousness. When you see yourself operating as an elite specialist in the Lord's Army, you plan, prepare, and live differently. Our mission is to go into all the world and take back from the enemy what belongs to God. We do this by penetrating all spheres of society to influence and demonstrate the rule and reign of God through our attitudes, choices, and lifestyles.

You must discover your assignment and identify the sphere of influence God has called you to. This is where you will have grace, gifting, and favor to carry out your objective. It is important to realize that all men are on a journey. We are being trained and equipped for the next level in this quest. You move through life in seasons, and the way you prepare and live in one season qualifies you for promotion in the next. There is a cycle to taking dominion in life, and it starts with serving where you are today.

Many men fall into the trap of the Christian nice guy and are waiting for the big opportunity or invitation to drop down from heaven. Even when a man is destined for big things, the example we see in scripture always starts small.

WHAT'S IN YOUR HAND?

When Moses is chosen as the deliverer, his first reaction is fear. He immediately produces a list of reasons why he is not qualified. The Lord's question to Moses is, "What's in your hand?" Moses responds, "A staff." The Lord commands Moses to throw it down and shows him how he will use what's in his hand to fulfill his call.

God has already equipped you with everything you need to take the first step in your leadership journey and move into the enemy's territory to reclaim the ground for God's Kingdom. When David is raised up to fight Goliath, he takes inventory of what is in his hand: a slingshot. This shepherd's sling will be used to slay a giant and restore a nation.

When you weaponize, one of the first questions to answer is, "What's in my hand?" You have been equipped with God-given desires, natural talents, acquired skill sets, and spiritual gifts to help you accomplish everything in your assignment. We all are part of God's eternal purpose. Within this purpose lies a unique and specific calling over your life. Inside the Standard 59 Mastermind, we equip you with tools and frameworks to discover where God is leading you and what problem you are being raised up to solve.

SPIRITUAL AUTHORITY

After Jesus delivered the sermon on the mount, the Bible records that the crowds were amazed at His teaching, for He was teaching them as one having authority, not as their scribes. As a believer, you have access to authority when you walk in right standing with God. Unlocking your full authority and learning how to weaponize it for use in the Kingdom will take deliberate training.

NATURAL AUTHORITY

Your partnership is required to weaponize your gift mix. There is a role for the acquisition of new skills, honing your communication, and mastering your craft. As followers of Jesus, we do not place our trust in our training alone because we have an unfair advantage: the anointing of the Holy Spirit. When your preparation for your assignment meets God's favor and anointing on your mission, you become an unstoppable force. As mature men of God, we seek to acquire the skill sets needed for our assignment and work with diligence to develop authority where we are called to conduct business.

We use other actions and training to weaponize our authority and gift mix for the assignments we are called to complete. The mission of Standard 59 is to equip and empower you in your assignment by activating your spiritual gifts.

WEAPONIZE SUMMARY

You are charged with being a protector and guarding what God assigns you, just as Adam was charged to guard the garden.

There is an ongoing spiritual battle over the territory that rightfully belongs to God, and it is imperative that you learn to walk in your authority and be empowered by the Holy Spirit to take territory.

Accessing your God-given authority through deliberate training is a non-negotiable for fulfilling your assignment. This will require you to upgrade your mindset and see yourself as a warrior as you put on your armor and put off old ways of civilian thinking.

Your responsibility begins with understanding how to participate effectively in battle. This starts with praying effectively, asking for direction and blessing, and then taking action, starting with what's in your hand.

OPTIMIZE
OPTIMIZING YOUR FAITH, FAMILY, FITNESS AND FINANCES

How does growth take place? The answers to these questions are in breaking down the necessary actions to achieve the goal into their most minor components. How do you get in shape? You get in shape one meal at a time, further broken down to one bite at a time. How do you build muscle? You stimulate new muscle growth one workout at a time and one rep at a time. You grow in anything by repetition and training. You must put your reps in.

How does Joshua take the Promised Land? The Lord tells him that everywhere his foot will tread will belong to Israel (Joshua 1:3). For Joshua, it's one step at a time. It's a step-by-step process. Joshua and the nation of Israel have the legal authority to occupy the promised land, but they still must enter it to possess it. There is action necessary, and they will take their territory step by step.

Walking with Christ to obtain the promises that you have legal access to works the same spiritually for you as it did for Joshua naturally: step by step. Spiritual growth mirrors physical growth in the natural realm. Most of the time, it doesn't look noticeable until one day, it does. There are times we experience accelerated growth, but usually, it is a very slow, step-by-step process, 1% at a time. Walking is the pattern we are provided in scripture. "Walk in the spirit and you will not fulfill the lust of the flesh." Walking is a metaphor for life and signifies incremental progress. Every step you take is a new achievement.

Earlier in this book, I told you that the growth that God desires in us is not automatic and doesn't happen by accident. This type of growth will demand your full intention. Being born into a family as a son is only the start of your sonship. Sonship comes with responsibility and being intentional about your growth into the full expression of God's plan for you.

This is what it means to reach your full potential and full stature as a man of God (Ephesians 4:13). So why are some men stuck and stagnant, with no growth and no fruit in their lives? If you're not seeing growth in your life, it's because you never fully intended to grow.

In the parable of the soil, Jesus describes what happens when the seed lands on four different types of soil.

1. Some seed falls beside the road and is stolen and eaten by birds.
2. Some seed falls on rocky ground, it immediately springs up and then withers because there is no depth for the roots to go.
3. Some seed falls among thorns and gets choked out, so it doesn't yield any fruit.
4. Some seed falls on good ground and has the potential to yield a 30, 60, or 100-fold return.

Many Christians are living their life passively, expecting God to do everything for them. The Christian nice guy who is stuck in Ditch 1 has an expectation that "God does everything for me." On the other side of the road, we find the Orphan Alpha mentality that claims, "I do it all myself." Both mindsets lack the true revelation of God's process. Scripture repeatedly warns us that we should grow from glory to glory, moving from level to level in life. The man who bears 30, 60, or a 100-fold result in life must know how to partner with God's process for growth.

THE PERFECT VS. PERMISSIVE WILL OF GOD

Have you ever wondered what the difference is between the man who produces a 30—or 60-fold return and the man who sees a 100-fold return? The answer lies in understanding God's perfect and permissive will for your life. In Romans 12:2, we discover that the main reason we must renew our minds is to prove God's good, acceptable, and perfect will for our lives. Notice three facets of God's will:

- God's Good Will

- God's Acceptable Will
- God's Perfect Will

God desires you to reach your full growth, achieve your full potential, and receive your full reward. A 100-fold return is no less than His perfect will for you.

Not everything you experience in life is God's perfect will. Your free will can easily override His perfect plan and lead you to do things you desire that are not His highest will for you based on the choices you make. Some of your choices can fall under His permissive will. It may be good and acceptable, but it is not His perfect will for you. God may allow it and even bless you, but you will never produce 100-fold if it's not His perfect will. For example, God's will in the Old Testament was He would govern Israel as their King, Lawgiver and Judge, but the nation desired to be like other nations and demanded a King to rule over them. This was never His perfect plan, but because the people desired a King, He conceded and gave them what they wanted.

PARTNERSHIP

When you study the language of the Bible, you will see a shift from servants and slaves to sons and friends. The New Testament provides another term critical to understanding your role in God's process. In Hebrews 3:14, we read that "we have become partakers with Christ…" That word, partaker, is more accurately translated as 'partner.' T. Austin Sparks states that the correct translation of Hebrews 3:14 reads like this:

"We are become partners with Christ if we hold fast the beginning of our confidence firm unto the end."

Partnership is the path to God's perfect will. When a man partners with God, that man's attitude and actions shift.
- Christian Nice Guys say, "God does it for me"

- Orphan Alphas say, "I do it myself"
- Kingdom Driven Men are Partners who declare, "I do it with God"

God always uses a man when he wants to bring a solution to the earth. It's imperative that you understand that without God, you can't accomplish anything. Your own willpower and strength will fall short. Without your partnership, God won't move in and through you. He requires your surrender, commitment, and intention in His process.

WITHOUT GOD, YOU CAN'T WITHOUT YOU, HE WON'T

God can't fulfill your potential for you because you are required to partner with His process. Partnership is cooperation with God; it's where you co-operate. Jesus first invites you into communion with Him and then imparts an assignment to co-labor with Him to fulfill the great commission. Partnership is:

- Co-union
- Co-labor
- Co-operation
- Co-mission

What does partnership look like in scripture? F.B. Meyer describes it like this.

- *The walls of Jericho could only fall down by divine power- but the children of Israel must assemble and march around them*
- *God created the seed – man must plow, sow, reap, thresh, and grind*
- *Only Jesus could multiply the loaves – but man must provide the bread*
- *Only Jesus could raise the dead- but man must roll away the stone.*
- *Only God can remove difficulties that block a blessed life but man must obey the commands and fulfill the duties that God has instructed us to walk in.*

> *There are things you should do – that you are not doing*
> *There are things you shouldn't do - that you are doing*

The danger is doing before or doing more than God instructed. Don't scale the walls you are supposed to march around, and don't shout before God has given the word.

You optimize your life through partnership with the Lord. Optimize is defined as *"an act, process, or methodology of making something as fully perfect, functional, or effective as possible."*

The four domains we focus on inside Standard 59 are our faith, family, fitness, and finances. Partnership with God in every area of our lives is the goal and the solution.

FAITH

As you optimize your spiritual growth, you progress through different levels. Each stage of development has different needs. The Apostle John teaches us that we progress from children to young men to fathers (1 John 2:12-14). The danger is when you never experience growth and get stuck in an infant stage. We see this can happen in the warnings written in the book of Hebrews; the author instructs the readers that they should be mature enough to eat meat, but they still have to receive milk because of their immaturity.

Milk is for babies. Meat is for men.

MASTER YOUR MIND

The Apostle prays in 3 John 2 that you may prosper and be in good health, just as your soul prospers. Soul prosperity happens within your mind, your will, and your emotions. Transformation occurs when we renew our minds. Changing our beliefs is the first step to a new mindset. Scripture teaches that the mind set on the spirit is life (Romans 8:5,6), and as we think, we become (Proverbs 23:7). We rewire our beliefs and renew our minds by thinking, speaking, and choosing, followed by our actions, which determine the results we have in life. This process starts with what we believe.

The average man has around 60,000 thoughts per day. Those thoughts provide a soundtrack with a playlist of our self-talk. When you repeat the same thoughts, it is called meditation. Every man meditates. The question is not whether you meditate. The real question is, what are you meditating on? The story of Joshua presents us with a key to optimizing our faith. A close examination of the Lord's instructions to Joshua reveals them to be a map guiding him to total success in his mission. The power source enabling Joshua to carry out all required of him is Biblical Meditation.

"This book of the law shall not depart from your mouth, but you shall meditate on it day and night..."

Joshua 1:8

THE POWER OF MEDITATION

In Psalm 1, we see the attributes and actions of the blessed man. The word "blessed" is translated as fortunate, prosperous, and favored by God. The catalyst for this soul prosperity is habitual biblical meditation. Psalm 1 shows you that when you habitually meditate on biblical teachings and precepts, you will see five shifts in your life.

1. You will be like a tree firmly planted
2. You will be fed by streams of water
3. You will yield fruit in your season at the proper time
4. Your leaf will not wither or fall off
5. And in whatever you do, you succeed and prosper

We optimize our faith through various methods to strengthen our spirit, and master our mind.

FAMILY

YOUR MARRIAGE

God created man because he wanted a partner to represent Himself on the earth. When God created woman for man, He was providing you, as a man, with your counterpart and a partner in life. The word 'helper' that God uses to describe Eve, is also used throughout scripture of God. God is depicted as our helper just as he fashioned our wives to be our 'helpers.'

Man is formed from the dust of the ground, but the woman is taken from the side of Adam. This presents a picture of a side-by-side partnership. As a husband, you are to provide leadership for your wife the same way Christ leads us. The leadership style Jesus models is servant leadership. Jesus is a leader who self-sacrifices for His bride and expects us as men to do the same for our wives.

"Husbands, love your wives, just as Christ also loved the church and gave Himself up for her,"

Ephesians 5:25.

As men we are responsible for the results we have in our marriage. The law of sowing and reaping is not only for your money. Whatever you sow into your marriage will be what you reap as the result of your relationship. As a man, you are a builder. One of the ways you create and build is with your words. What you think influences what you speak, and what you speak builds an atmosphere around you and in your home. What is the atmosphere you have built? What is the energy you bring into your house, marriage, and family when you walk in after a day's work? You are reaping today what you sowed yesterday. If you don't like the results of your relationship, watch your words and change what you say.
The most powerful way to shift the atmosphere of your marriage is to

pray for your wife. We have developed a practice within Standard 59 where we pray over our wives. The rule we implemented was to lay our hand on our wife physically and pray and bless her out loud. When the men do this, the reports that come back are always amazing. Greater spiritual intimacy leads to intimacy in all areas of marriage. If you want to build a stronger marriage, start by demonstrating your ability to lead your wife by being a man she can trust and become a safe place for her. My challenge for you is to pray over your wife today.

YOUR FAMILY

Family is God's design and is a model to demonstrate God's vision for our relationship with Him. A properly aligned and functioning family is the bedrock of a strong society. The foundation of every family starts with the father. The root of the word father means foundation. In Deuteronomy 6, The Lord provides the blueprint and instructions for the family. The foundation for the way we lead our families is found in Deuteronomy 6:5, where you are commanded to:

"Love the LORD your God with all your heart and with all your soul and with all your might."

From this starting point, our leadership will be ordered and aligned. Fathers impart identity and mothers create the atmosphere where that identity can grow, be nurtured, and be expressed in its full potential. As fathers, intentionally leading our families is more than just Biblical wisdom; it's a command that comes with the confidence that when we follow the Lord's instruction, there are promises that will be realized in our family's lives. As fathers, we are instructed to diligently teach the Lord's commands to our children.

"You shall teach them diligently to your sons and shall talk of them when you sit in your house and when you walk by the way and when you lie down and when you rise up."

Deuteronomy 6:7

The goal for fathers is to raise children who will serve the Lord and know how to lead themselves by teaching and transferring leadership lessons, virtues, and disciplines to succeed and lead in life. God's vision to bring light to the nations and transform culture is not a top-down approach; it's a bottom-up strategy that starts with how you, as a man, lead your family. Kingdom Driven Men make a stand in the midst of culture and declare with their words and their actions:

"...But as for me and my house, we will serve the LORD."
Joshua 24:15

I view my role as a father as not 'just' raising children. My wife and I are committed to raising giant killers who will serve the Lord, set people free, and take territory for the Kingdom of God. Like arrows in the hand of a warrior, they will hit the target (Psalm 127:4).

FITNESS

The temple in the Old Testament was a wonder to behold. It was meticulously crafted with the finest materials and with God providing the most minute measurements. So much time, effort, and planning went into designing and building the physical temple. In the New Testament, you are referred to as the temple of the Holy Spirit.

One of our primary calls as men is to guard and protect. You do not need to be a competitive bodybuilder, crossfitter, or powerlifter to prove your masculinity. But you should be physically capable of defending yourself and your family, which can not occur unless you steward your physical temple. It has become too common in Christianity to hyper-focus on spiritual growth while ignoring practical stewardship of our natural resources, including our strength and energy. Physical exercise is profitable, serves a purpose, and is key to having an optimized experience in your life. To be the man God created you to be, you must optimize your body and manage your energy so you can fulfill your mission to protect your family and your call to work.

DELIBERATE DISCOMFORT

Today's modern man lives a comfortable life. We are surrounded by amenities that kings and queens throughout history have never had the privilege of. We live and work in climate-controlled environments where efficiencies have minimized almost all physical effort. This sedentary lifestyle has resulted in chronic conditions that keep men from moving. The only remedy to the environment that has made us soft and weak is to seek out deliberate discomfort.

You are built to thrive under pressure and challenge. Without challenge, you become passive and weak, ensuring that when you do face a real challenge, you will fail under the pressure. Embracing a lifestyle of deliberate discomfort is not limited to physical benefits; you build your mental fortitude whenever you challenge yourself physically. I believe all men should have some form of strength training in their schedule. Strength training develops the mental fortitude to meet all resistance with force.

Inside Standard 59, we equip men with a library of health optimization and fitness resources and programs to take on challenges and experience growth. One core agreement we honor is that we intentionally move every day. This could be a strength training session, endurance training, or an intentional walk to meet a daily steps goal. Regardless of your exercise choice, you need to steward your physical temple. This means moving daily and getting high-quality fuel sources to optimize your living experience.

Physical training is the ultimate metaphor for life. The push and pull followed by the rest and the recovery period is a reflection of life. Struggling, pushing and pressing against resistance develops discipline and is how transformation happens.

Although our faith is our priority, I have observed a link between my spiritual walk and physical discipline and diligence. My experience is that when I am sloppy in one area of life, it carries over into others. On the flip side, when I am structured and disciplined in my fitness, sleep, and eating habits, there is a direct correlation to my spiritual disciplines and walk with the Lord.

If you cut corners with your training you must ask, where else am I cutting corners in life? Kingdom Driven Men know:

The way you do ANYTHING is the way you do EVERYTHING.

BREATHE

Optimization doesn't stop with training. We employ strategies to minimize stress and prime our bodies to meet and receive from the Lord in our tent of meeting. One of those practices is biblical breathing. To receive free training on how to implement this powerful practice into your daily life, visit Biblicalbreathing.com.

FINANCE

One of the biggest battles you will face is over money. This subject is full of contention and misunderstanding. More than 2,300 Bible verses on money, wealth, and possessions exist. The orphan mindset manifests in how you handle your money. I have met many men who have large bank accounts with a poverty mindset. Fear of lack holds many in a grip of working to over-accumulate. The Bible states that a man who is only driven to accumulate based on growing his holdings so he can build bigger barns and have a better life is a fool (Luke 12:16-21).

In the Kingdom of God, we are not owners. We are stewards. The major shift that you need to embrace when you follow God is that you own nothing. We are given gifts and entrusted with resources to work, invest, and multiply for the Kingdom of God. The powerful illustration Jesus provides is in the parable of the talents. Talent in the context of this parable is a measurement of money, not gifting, although you are also a steward of your natural talents as well. The lesson for you is that God lends to you as an investor and expects a return on His investment. Stewardship is defined as conducting, supervising, or managing something entrusted to one's care. The stewards in the parable of the talents are expected to manage and multiply what was entrusted to them.

In the Old Testament, Kings went to war, and after they conquered an enemy army, they came back with the spoils of war. They gave to God's work from this war chest and supported the Levitical priesthood. In a similar fashion, you have been equipped to go into the world and wage war through your work. You have been given the ability and power to create wealth (Deuteronomy 8:18). You serve and earn as an entrepreneur or in an organization that solves a problem in exchange for value. Your dominion mandate is to co-labor with God and influence within the marketplace. You are entrusted as a steward to manage and multiply what God has placed in your hand.

The book of Proverbs instructs us that a wise man leaves an inheritance to his children's children. Leaving a legacy like this does not happen by accident. Understand that there is a war over finances. The ruler of this world opposes God's people over every inch of territory, which represents a loss to the kingdom of darkness. No one goes to war without a strategy. There are strategies, tactics, and tools that the top 1% use to protect, preserve, and grow their wealth that the average man on Main Street is unaware of.

Every man needs a Kingdom wealth war map—a plan to follow and a map to understand where he is and where he's heading. Inside the Standard 59 Mastermind, we equip you with Kingdom wealth-building principles to show you proven paths to building walls to protect your wealth and then growing with a well-planned strategy.

CONCLUSION

In this chapter, I have included a small sample of what we have put into practice in our quest to optimize our Faith, Family, Fitness, and Finances. Kingdom Driven Men are committed to growth and optimizing the following four domains through partnership with God. To fully optimize and walk in your calling, you must stop trying and start training. Inside the Standard 59 Mastermind you get a plan to win in the following areas.

Endnotes:
Sparks, T. Austin
"Partnership with Christ" From "A Witness and A Testimony" magazines, 1936-1937, Vol. 14-5 - 15-3. https://www.austin-sparks.net

Meyer, F.B.
"Joshua and the Land of Promise" Copyright © 1893 Fleming H. Revell Company edited for 3BSB by Baptist Bible Believer in the spirit of the Colportage Ministry of a century ago
www.baptistbiblebelievers.com

FAITH

We are called to be overcomers, and we are more than conquerors. We must learn to fight and run our race like elite competitive athletes, enforcing our victory. We embrace transformation in our character and conduct through the cross. We build our lives on the centrality and supremacy of Jesus Christ.

FAMILY

We are committed husbands and dedicated fathers. Honor bleeds through all of our relationships. We create the culture in our homes and carry the responsibility of leading our families through the challenges and victories in life. We are the example, and we raise the standard by creating generational impact through our leadership.

FITNESS

We chase goals and relentlessly pursue excellence in all things. We understand that first, we are called to lead ourselves, and that includes stewarding our physical capacity. If we cannot function at a high level, meeting the daily demands in the various roles we are called to operate in, everything will suffer.

FINANCE

We are businessmen. We embrace work and understand our call to the marketplace. Advance and occupy is our mandate. We are not ashamed or apologize for the value we create or for receiving the reward of our labors. We are called to enlarge our borders and expand our territory for the Kingdom.

OPTIMIZE SUMMARY

Growth takes place 1% at a time. Your spiritual growth is depicted as walking in the Spirit. This represents incremental growth and progress. You optimize your growth by upgrading your operating system and practicing daily disciplines.

God's goal for you is that you live within His perfect will and produce a 100-fold return. Fulfilling your dominion mandate will require your partnership with God. Partnership with God is an active participation in His process.

One powerful way we optimize our spiritual walk is by practicing Biblical meditation. Every man meditates. The question is, what are you meditating on? Biblical meditation is commanded and practiced by every powerful man being used to advance God's Kingdom.

You are called to facilitate growth in your marriage and family. As you embrace your call to leadership, you optimize your role as a husband and father, leading in your marriage and your family by your example and instruction.

You are the temple of the Holy Spirit and must exhibit stewardship of your physical being. It is your responsibility to raise the standard in your fitness and manage your energy.

Creating wealth and stewarding your finances is part of your dominion mandate to conquer and subdue. In the Kingdom, you are not an owner but a steward responsible for producing a return on investment.

PART IV:
UPGRADE YOUR ENVIRONMENT

TRUE TRANSFORMATION
THE FOUR CORNERSTONES FOR TRUE TRANSFORMATION

You have just been equipped with the Kingdom Driven Order and a sample of some principles and practices you can implement right now. Before attempting to apply what you have learned, there are four cornerstones that must be set to encounter true transformation. Without these firmly in place, attempts to implement the Kingdom Driven Order would be like trying to construct a formidable castle on a foundation made of sand.

1. TELL THE TRUTH

Jesus always brings men to honesty. In Matthew 6, Jesus issues a warning to men by calling out the hypocrites. He illustrates the danger of living a lie. Hypocrites are synonymous with actors who take the stage and pretend they are something they are not. The first step when approaching God is to understand that He requires you to tell the truth. Adam hid himself from the Lord's presence when he sinned in the garden. The question that the Lord asks Adam echoes through eternity, Adam…

"WHERE ARE YOU?"

The all-knowing creator did not ask this question for His benefit. The power of His question illustrates the first step in being reconciled to God and enrolling in His process to encounter true transformation. All progress starts with telling the truth. In Psalm 15, David asks, "Who can abide with the Lord?" The answer is "He who walks with integrity, and works righteousness, and speaks truth in his heart He does not slander with his tongue." In Proverbs 6, a lying tongue is one of the seven things God hates.

Jesus is the way, the truth, and the life. An encounter with Jesus requires that you stop lying, stand in the truth of where you are today, and own your circumstances. It is from this point that progress can take place. Just like Adam, you must come clean and answer honestly to the Creator's question; "WHERE ARE YOU?"

2. HONOR YOUR WORD

The next step is to honor your word. In the Old Testament, the commandment is "You shall be careful to perform what goes out from your lips, just as you have voluntarily vowed to the LORD your God, what you have promised" (Deuteronomy 23:23). The standard stays the same in the New Testament with John teaching "but whoever keeps His word, in him the love of God has truly been perfected. By this we know that we are in Him: the one who says he abides in Him ought himself to walk in the same manner as He walked" (1 John 2:5-6).

When you tell the truth, you take off your mask and stop lying to yourself and those around you by being honest with yourself and God. The fastest way to step into your masculine mandate and exhibit leadership in life is by doing what you said you would do. This is the definition of integrity; you must stay in integrity through the process of transformation.

3. VISION

After encountering Jesus, you need to get a GDV (God Driven Vision) and have a clear view of your destination, your calling, and the expectation that God will fulfill His plan for your life with your surrender. Faith is an earnest expectation, belief and trust that God will transform you into who He created you to be. While many men live complacent and passive lives while waiting to get to heaven, Kingdom Driven Men live differently. We walk with a view that we don't have to wait to die to experience eternal life now. The promise of Jesus is that those who place their complete belief and trust in Him will not die but experience eternal life and live out of this new source of life now.

4. EXCELLENCE

Excellence is a requirement throughout the process of transformation. The Apostle Peter states that God, through His divine power has supplied us with promises that empower us to be partners with Him (2 Peter 1:4). What is required from us is that we apply excellence. The word in Greek is 'Arete,' and is translated as a virtuous course of thought, feeling and action. This is moral excellence.

GOD SUPPLIES - YOU APPLY

God supplies grace, and you apply excellence. Excellence is where your intention meets your effort. We are not exhibiting effort to get saved or stay saved but we are applying effort and intention in our walk as a disciple, excellence in the disciplines, practices and virtues of Biblical manhood. As Dallas Willard teaches, "Grace is not opposed to effort, it is opposed to earning. Earning is an attitude. Effort is an action."

"For by these He has granted to us His precious and magnificent promises, so that by them you may become partakers of the divine nature, having escaped the corruption that is in the world by lust. Now for this very reason also, applying all diligence, in your faith supply moral excellence, and in your moral excellence, knowledge, and in your knowledge, self-control, and in your self-control, perseverance, and in your perseverance, godliness, and in your godliness, brotherly kindness, and in your brotherly kindness, love. For if these qualities are yours and are increasing, they render you neither useless nor unfruitful in the true knowledge of our Lord Jesus Christ."

2 Peter 1:4-8

Through the process of your transformation you must maintain excellence in your attitude and practice.

EXCELLENCE DOES NOT TOLERATE MEDIOCRITY

In the next chapter, I will show you the one thing most men miss. Without this, you will never be able to encounter true transformation.

Dallas Willard
THE GREAT OMISSION: Reclaiming Jesus' Essential Teachings on Discipleship p. 61
Copyright 2006 HarperCollins

THE MISSING INGREDIENT
UPGRADE YOUR ENVIRONMENT

There is a secret within the Godhead that provides the pattern for us. God exists within community. Before the foundation of the world, the Father, the Son, and the Holy Spirit were in communion with each other. When God created the earth and placed Adam in the garden, His vision for His new creation was to start a family. Every species has an environment where it grows, survives, and thrives. The natural habitat of this new creation species is with each other.

God's plan for man is interdependence over independence. Satan is the original orphan who chose independence from God. This is why he works overtime to keep you separated from your natural habitat. There is a battle to keep you isolated and away from the environment where you thrive. In John 10:10, Jesus warns us, "The thief comes only to steal and kill and destroy…" If he can't kill you, he will seek to destroy you, and his sights are fixed on annihilating your identity.

In the Old Testament, the evil king Manasseh takes captives of Israel. He does not outwardly slaughter them. Instead, he disperses them across different lands, separating them from their community and their environment.

He doesn't kill them, but he KILLS THEIR IDENTITY

When Daniel and his friends find themselves in Babylon under the rule of King Nebuchadnezzar, the first thing their captors do is assign them Babylonian names. The goal is to strip them of their identity. The enemy and the world are always seeking to rob you of your true identity in Christ. He doesn't have to kill you to kill your identity; he attacks you by removing you from your people. Your environment.

AVOID ISOLATION

God called you to separate, not isolate. The image of the masculine hero many of us were given to emulate is the lone wolf. This has been presented through stories, movies, and media. Lone wolves are independent, strong and capable, and they always work alone. We have bought the lie of the lone wolf, shaping our expectations of how we are to play the game and win in life.

The trap of the lone wolf is very real as you progress through the seasons of life. Priorities shift, friend circles change, and time becomes a commodity. Time invested with friends is now replaced with work, and time spent on recreation has been replaced with your kid's activities and obligations. It takes more intention to connect with others. There are 1,000 reasons why it's more convenient not to connect with other men.

CHANGE YOUR LOCATION

When Jesus assembles his team, the first thing He does is invite His disciples into a new environment. They are required to leave their familiar way of life and become immersed in a new environment. The culture of the Kingdom of God is community.

Whenever God prepares a man for promotion, He changes that man's location.

- Joseph must go to Egypt to enter the process that will lead to his promotion
- Moses must leave Egypt to go into the wilderness to be prepared for his promotion
- Jesus must leave Nazareth to step into His mission and ministry at the appointed time
- The disciples must leave their known way of life to be trained before they change the world

What's the key to real transformation?

- Transformation doesn't just happen with **INFORMATION**.
- Transformation cannot be maintained through **MOTIVATION**.
- Transformation is **NEVER** done in **ISOLATION**.

UPGRADE YOUR ENVIRONMENT

You must upgrade your environment. Changing your environment is a biblical principle; we now have the science to prove it. The latest research on encountering transformation in any area of your life points to being in the right environment.

If you ever started a diet and then broke it by binge eating while watching Netflix, or you made a New Year's resolution, but within three months you gave up on it… it's because you never upgraded your environment. The fact is you don't change through an event. No one ever has because change is not an event. It is a process. And the process only works when you change your environment because true transformation happens in a community.

God's plan for us is **KINGDOM COMMUNITY** and **BROTHERHOOD**; the enemy's plan is **isolation** and **distraction**.

Traditional approaches, while well-intentioned, fall short of producing the transformation required for us to step fully into our roles as powerful, KINGDOM DRIVEN leaders. The pervasive issues of identity confusion, lack of confidence, and life's distractions have held men in cycles of defeat, far from the dominion we're called to take and the impact we're called to make. But there is a way forward.

WHAT'S NEXT?
THE STANDARD 59 MASTERMIND

In this book, I have made you aware of the enemies you will face in your quest to fulfill your dominion mandate and equipped you with the KINGDOM-DRIVEN ORDER. This framework will bring you into order and alignment with God's will and plan so you can dominate in life. My goal with this book was to hand you these high-level strategies you can implement immediately into your daily operating system.

But despite the information you have been equipped with, most men will do nothing. Doing nothing comes with a cost that you and others around you pay. What does it cost you NOT to implement the Kingdom Driven Order?

DOING NOTHING COMES WITH A COST

If you never **ALIGN** with who God says you are, you get stuck in cycles of PMS. Pain followed by self-medication and then shame at behaviors that don't align with your identity. The root of many of the painful problems you are dealing with relates back to missing identity-based training.

If you never **DESIGN** your life by disabling distractions and implementing a system to dominate your day, you stay stuck in cycles of starting and never finishing. The price you pay is overwhelm, stress, chaos and living with the disappointment that you don't finish what you start.

If you never **WEAPONIZE** and learn to access your authority, you miss the empowerment necessary to take your territory. The price you pay is not fulfilling your assignment with the tools necessary to stop the enemy's attacks.

If you never learn to **OPTIMIZE** through partnership with God, you will never raise the standard in your faith, family, fitness, and finances.

The price you pay is that you will continue to struggle in one or more of these areas.

If you never **BUILD BROTHERHOOD** or connect in a community, you remain a lone wolf. The price you pay is staying isolated and prone to loneliness and attack with no support or community.

Doing nothing always comes with a cost. The next option is to do it yourself.

DO IT YOURSELF?

You can try to implement this order in your life on your own, which is extremely challenging. Or you can take the proven path with guidance and brotherhood and join us inside The Standard 59 Mastermind.

I have participated in men's Bible studies and shopped for a cohort of men representing the values of the Kingdom, centered on the deeper Christian life and not the 'be the best version of yourself' superficial Christianity. I could not find anyone doing what I was looking for, so I created an environment for men committed to Raising the Standard.

WHAT IS THE STANDARD 59 MASTERMIND?

I founded the Standard 59 Mastermind for men who are ready to upgrade their environment, step into leadership, build kingdom brotherhood, and install a new operating system to change their lives.

We are a no-nonsense community of KINGDOM DRIVEN MEN who are committed to raising the standard in our faith, family, fitness and finances. If you join us, I can promise you will get results much quicker than if you try to do this alone.

Inside the Standard 59 Mastermind, you get a proven path to unlock your full potential with clear outcomes.

Create Your GOD DRIVEN VISION: You will build your GDV to get clarity and take territory. Discover your purpose, define your mission and walk in your assignment. Your God Driven Vision Plan will clearly outline your goals, priorities, and actions in the four key areas of life.

Develop DISCIPLINE and Self-Mastery: Build an Unshakable and Anti-Fragile Identity. You will build your individual leadership by implementing actions with systems. Get equipped to be a disciple who takes responsibility with unwavering commitment.

BUILD Your Kingdom WEALTH WAR MAP: Co-Create your personal wealth plan tailored to fit your income level and goals. These Kingdom strategies will focus on protecting and growing your wealth so you can MAXIMIZE your financial life and leave a legacy.

Build Your FOCUS and FLOW: Learn how to Dominate Your Day and design systems for Kingdom productivity. Your mission will require your focus. Get these strategies and daily practices to build and access flow states for unparalleled productivity.

LEAD Your FAMILY: Be The Husband and Father who leads by modeling, training, and serving your wife and children with integrity and excellence. Get strategies and training to connect with your wife, and learn how to biblically lead your family.

Communicate with CONFIDENCE: Build self-awareness and boost your E.Q. Get equipped with skills to connect with others quickly, exert Influence, and lead without authority. Learn how to establish trust and communicate powerfully.

Access Your AUTHORITY: Get trained on how to walk in your God Given Authority to create atmospheres with your actions and presence. Understand and unlock your motivational and spiritual gifts to fulfill your mission.

OPTIMIZE Your FITNESS: Get equipped with a plan and the tools to manage your energy, burn fat, and build muscle. Become the protector of your family by being the example and fuel your mission in optimal health.

WHO IS THIS FOR?

This is for ambitious Christian men and driven high performers who are ready to raise the standard and be the man God created them to be. This is for you if you want:

MORE Connection with God, Taking Dominion, Fulfilling Your Potential, Favor in the Marketplace, Promotion in Business, Reaching Your Calling, and Operating in Your Purpose.

LESS of the Chaos Within, Inner Conflict, Strife at Home, Stress at Work, Feeling Disconnected with Faith and Shame at Behaviors That Don't Align with Your True Identity.

Inside the Standard 59 Mastermind, we have developed protocols, practices and tools that power our lives.

WE DON'T 'TRY.' WE 'TRAIN.'

Inside you will get equipped with a process that creates progress. I will warn you, this isn't for passive Christian men who are satisfied with superficial Christianity.

This is for you if you are committed to growth and want to experience transformation and walk with Jesus in a close relationship with power.

If you're ready to BE THE MAN God created you to be, join us here: https://www.standard59.com/mastermind

Or message me the word KINGDOM to Josh@standard59.com

LEAD. FIGHT. WIN.

JOSH

A NO NONSENSE COMMUNITY OF KINGDOM DRIVEN MEN

CONNECTING WITH GOD, MASTERING THEIR MIND, MULTIPLYING THEIR FINANCES, TAKING DOMINION

MASTERMIND

JOIN THE BROTHERHOOD
WWW.STANDARD59MASTERMIND.COM

THE MAN WHO WROTE THE BOOK

Josh Khachadourian is a husband, father, coach and host of the **'Raising The Standard'** podcast. Josh has spent the past 20 years ascending the corporate ladder in a Fortune 100 company, where he has built high-performing teams and developed best-in-class leaders. Josh's passion is to help men implement biblical systems with Kingdom principles so they can expand and prosper in all areas.

Follow On Facebook & Instagram:
@kingdomathlete

Subscribe To The YouTube Channel:
@RaisingTheStandard

BOOK JOSH TO SPEAK AT YOUR NEXT EVENT

Josh speaks and trains on a variety of topics. Inquire about speaking and podcast interviews by emailing:
Josh@standard59.com

ARE YOU READY TO TAKE DOMINION IN LIFE WITH JESUS AS THE STANDARD?

Listen to the Raising The Standard Podcast to Get Weekly Motivation for the Kingdom Driven Man

 LEVEL UP IN LIFE WITH A BLUEPRINT FOR YOU AS A KINGDOM MAN

 STEP INTO BIBLICAL MASCULINITY WITH THE RIGHT DAILY ACTIONS

 GET STRATEGIES AND TACTICS ON HOW TO EXPAND THE KINGDOM OF GOD IN YOUR LIFE TODAY

www.ingramcontent.com/pod-product-compliance
Lightning Source LLC
LaVergne TN
LVHW020326100426
835512LV00043B/3355